Writers of Wales

Editors
MEIC STEPHENS   R. BRINLEY JONES

Brian Morris

HARRI WEBB

University of Wales Press

Cardiff 1993

I

Harri Webb is a writer who, for nearly fifty years, has had only one subject. That subject is Wales. For beginning with such a sweeping generalization which is also not entirely true, there is good reason. The Writers of Wales series exists to celebrate Welsh writers from many centuries and an infinite variety of backgrounds who have written extensively but not exclusively about their country. No one, in the more than three score and ten volumes in the series, has written about Wales more intensively, steadily, passionately, or with greater variety of approach, of genre, of style, than Harri Webb. As journalist, newspaper editor, pamphleteer, poet, essayist, scriptwriter for radio and television, media 'personality' and social and cultural historian, he has focused his articulate attention on the glories, the particularities and the plight of his nation. He makes few comparisons. Even as a poet he only occasionally presents Wales as the image of any larger community, utopian or oppressed. He is a writer *of* Wales in the sense that he writes almost obsessively *about* Wales and, for him, Wales is itself alone.

It is also significant that he is a writer by nature, and not simply with an eye for publication. From his adolescent years until quite recently he has intermittently kept a diary which, despite its chronological gaps, is a voluminous record of his life and times, written usually in a private and unselfconscious style without the slightest concern for posterity. He records in 1974 that the earliest of his diaries to have survived, from 1931 and 1933, his eleventh and thirteenth years, are little more than *a record of a busy, normal and happy family life*, but that, a few years later, the compulsion to chronicle became deeper and more insistent:

From the age of sixteen however I kept a diary of my school life, which obviously meant a great deal more to me than all the rest of my life put together, as it was exclusively an account of my school curriculum and such activities as plays, school trips, sports days etc. It ran, between 1936 and 1938, when I went up to Oxford, into twenty-four copy-books, the decently robust copy-books of those days, with the embossed covers of thick cardboard, and must have run, over the three years, into the best part of 200,000 words!

He adds that, re-reading them in middle life, he was so overwhelmed by their monumental tedium that he summarily got rid of them. The more continuous run of surviving diaries dates from 1942, but there are gaps until the latest 'series' begins, as a new start, in 1974. The diaries are all written in a crabbed, often almost illegible hand, and the entries vary from the most mundane record of diurnal events to self-communing more typical of the *journal intime*. He writes:

From time to time, however, I have succumbed to the temptation of keeping a fuller journal. These times, on the whole, have not been the good ones . . . They refer to states of mind which I now scarcely recognize, to 'decisions' which seemed of cosmic importance at the time, to people and places I have completely forgotten in the course of a varied life, whose changing scenes and milieux and preoccupations have effaced much.

The surviving diaries, part of an archive which is

2

held by his literary executor, amount to several hundred thousand words, and are an invaluable resource for biographers, historians, and critics of the future. They also testify to Harri Webb's almost atavistic urge to register both the quotidian events and the 'states of mind which I now scarcely recognize' in words. It has always been both natural and urgent for him that the things which concern him should be recorded. He writes: . . . *the earlier stages of my history must be set out, not in any sense as an exercise in autobiography, but merely 'for the record'.*

The distinction between autobiography and 'the record' is important. Harri Webb is anxious that the diaries should not be considered as in any way a history of himself, as a constructed work of art, an *apologia pro vita sua*, a text. The decision that they should survive rather than be destroyed seems to have been based on no clear sense of their being presented to any 'reader'. The concept of a 'readership' or any relationship between the reader and the text is something of which his mind seems utterly innocent. What matters is 'the record'. He uses the word not in its journalistic sense, where things are either 'on the record' or off it, but more in the way we speak of 'the fossil record' where the rocks provide an account in permanent form of facts or events, free of selection and free of judgement. Those of his private writings he has permitted to survive are, for him, part of the palimpsest of the culture of our time in Wales, and we may make of them what we will. He will not interfere. *Indeed*, he writes, *I am struck by how little relation my journals bear to anything I have written either in prose or verse, that has been deemed worth publishing or listening to.*

'The record' begins with the bare, historical, genea-
logical fact:

*I was born at 11.30 on the morning of Tuesday September 7th
1920, in the back bedroom of No 45 Tycoch Road, Swansea. My
father was William John Webb, third child and only son of John
Webb of High Pennard and his wife Elizabeth (Rees), a family
of small clifftop farmers. My mother was Lucy Irene Gibbs,
youngest of a large family born to John Gibbs, an estate worker
on the Kilvrough Estate, and his wife Elizabeth (Bowen) who
signed her name with a mark. Both my parents were in their
thirtieth year at the time of my birth.*

Even here, he cannot resist gilding the stark geneal-
ogy with the additional touches about his father's
family being 'clifftop' farmers, and his maternal
grandmother's probable illiteracy. Indeed, the matter
of literacy and language assumes importance at once.
Amongst his mother's family, his Auntie Mary was
married to Will Skinner, a big-boned, taciturn man, and
his uncle Davy John was the husband of *stern Auntie
Mary who never let their son Harry read the newspapers.*
Uncle William and Auntie Amelia *and their jolly
family* lived at Waunarlwydd, and the crucial point
for 'the record' is that this was Welsh-speaking
territory:

*Uncle William worked in the Garngoch No.3 pit and had picked
up the language there. Welsh was Auntie Amelia's first language, and this was the only one of the family homes where I
heard it. Their existence was more rural than industrial, they
had a big garden, almost a small-holding, kept a goat and lived
well. It was here I first tasted goose.*

Harri Webb's upbringing in Swansea, the Gower
peninsula and the adjacent areas suggests obvious
parallels with that of other articulate, English-

speaking Welshmen, like Dylan Thomas or Vernon Watkins. The rich and nourishing complex of town and country, industry and agriculture, sea and land, English and Welsh is common to them all: it provided a most powerful nurture in a close-knit society and a remarkably small area.

This is not to say that Harri Webb's earliest years were without reference to the wider world. His father was employed in the electricity works in the Strand, Swansea, and later, from 1935 to 1955, as a stoker and subsequently foreman in the Tir John power-station. His son recalls him cycling to work every night through the bombing of Swansea. Yet William Webb had emigrated to Australia as a young man, and worked on a sheep-farm near Perth. He served with the Anzac forces in the First World War, and took part in the Gallipoli landings. For years he kept up a correspondence with a family called Chandler at Subiaco, and told his son of his friendship with a Mr Peet, land agent of Boonooloo. Yet the boy's imagination was not nourished only by family facts about foreign parts. He has said that, at the age of eight, he read a novel by Major George Bruce, THE RAINBOW OF SABA, and it made a deep and lasting impression on him. And well it might, and well it may have informed many a later choice which Harri Webb made. It is a typical example of the boys' adventure-story, an historical romance of chivalry and daring, set around the Mediterranean, the Aral Sea, and Samarkand in the thirteenth century. It ends:

'Harold' she cried, 'the Blessing of the Rainbow said that Astura should never be without a Prince. Harold, my friend and true comrade – the only man I love – will you be the Prince?'

Such stuff as this prevents the shades of the prison-house from closing too early about the growing boy.

The Webbs moved to 58 Catherine Street, St Helens, Swansea, in 1922, and it was here that the happy, decently working-class parents brought up their only child. From 1927 to 1931 he was a pupil in the Oxford Street National School, now demolished, and in 1931 he went on to Glanmor Secondary Boys' School, which also no longer exists.

His school Report Book, covering the whole period 1931–38 has survived, and it paints a vivid picture. He seems to have taken no interest in any games, and under the heading 'Share in the Corporate Life of the School' for year after year there appears only the entry 'Dramatic Society'. From surviving programmes we know that he played Lady Percy in the school production of KING HENRY IV, Part I, in March 1934, Esther in John Drinkwater's A MAN'S HOUSE, in April 1936, and Lady Macbeth in February 1937, when he was in the sixth form. His academic progress is fully charted, term by term. He is nearly always in the first three in his form in English, French and Spanish, and his French master, in particular, loads him with praises in the age-old phraseology of school reports: 'an excellent pupil', 'very good work', and the like. He displays no talent for Art, Woodwork or Metalwork, and his performance in Arithmetic, Algebra and Geometry is deplorable. In the term ending 7 April, 1935, 'A.B.' (presumably his subject master) writes:

Absolutely feeble in Mathematics. Does not seem to apply himself to figures.

In the same term he comes first in English, first in French and second in Spanish, and the head master draws the moderately obvious conclusion:

Unfortunately it appears that his gift for languages is offset by great weakness in Mathematics.

However, with proper solicitude, he adds in the margin 'I am making an enquiry into this question, to see whether it is possible for something to be done'. Whether anything was done or not, it was to no effect, and Master Webb continued to be a complete mathematical duffer. In 1935, he passed the Central Welsh Board Examination with Distinction in English, Credits in History, French, Spanish and Biology, and dismal failure in all three mathematical disciplines. His years in the sixth form allowed him to indulge his 'gift for languages', in the study of English, French and Spanish, to such good effect that, in the term ending July, 1937, at the early age of sixteen years nine months, he passed all three subjects at what we would now call 'A level' with Credit. He stayed on for a third year in the sixth form, and was made a school prefect and (prophetically) Librarian. The final entry in his Report Book for the term ending July 8 1938, reads:

Heartiest congratulations upon his Open Exhibition of £80 at Magdalen College Oxford. W. Bryn Thomas, Head Master.

It was indeed a remarkable achievement, and brought him the addition of an LEA scholarship worth £40. He was the first pupil of Glanmor School ever to win an entrance exhibition at Oxford, and the school was given a half-day holiday in his honour. It is also noteworthy that his 'gift for languages' enabled him to learn sufficient Latin during the summer to fulfil the entrance conditions at Oxford. It was a rather strange curriculum at his Grammar School which permitted him to study Spanish to the highest level, while offering only Biology amongst the sciences, no Music, and neither Latin nor Greek.

So, equipped only with his talent for the tongues, Harri Webb was pitchforked from a Grammar School and the working-class streets of Swansea into Oxford, and pre-war Oxford at that, and into one of its most beautiful and impressive and fashionable Colleges, the College which still remembered Oscar Wilde as one of its alumni, as utterly English and bourgeois an environment as one could possibly imagine. The experience must have been a profound shock. There is almost nothing in the written record of his notes or diaries that refers to this period. He read the Honours school of Medieval and Modern Languages, specializing in French, Spanish and Portuguese. He seems to have taken part in some of the productions of the Magdalen College Dramatic Society, but nothing more. He himself says that he has no vivid memories of his undergraduate years, he seems to have made few friends and none with whom he kept in touch, and he appears to have studiously avoided the company of his compatriots. It may well be that the sudden exposure to Oxford was overwhelming, and it alienated him. To get there was a triumph, to be there was a disappointment. If so, it was an experience well known to his countrymen. Gwyn Thomas was subdued by Oxford, and he simply survived it, to become a distinguished Welsh writer in later years. The Welsh country lad, from humble origins, who flourished in Oxford's rarefied air, took a double First in Mods and Greats, and won the

Chancellor's Prize for an English essay, was Sir Lewis Morris, who went on to write a great deal, little of which is remembered. There may be a moral here, but it is certain that Oxford made almost no impression on Harri Webb, and he hardly ever refers to it in his writings.

In the summer vacation of 1939 Harri Webb's mother died, after a long illness. She is buried near the old home at Pennard. Her only son was particularly close to his mother, and her death affected him deeply. It may well have contributed to his disappointing performance in his final examinations. He was placed in the third division, and his father was certainly shocked and saddened by what he considered an unacceptable result. The rift between father and son dates from this period. Harri Webb never lived at home in Swansea again, and felt unable even to attend his father's funeral in 1956, though the event caused him deep grief, not unmixed with guilt at what he regarded as his part in the failure of the relationship.

On 26 August 1941 he was called up to serve in the Royal Navy. His Certificate of Service records that he was 5 ft 7 ins; Hair, D. Brown; Eyes, Brown; Complexion, Fresh; Marks, Wounds and Scars, Nil. Under 'Trade brought up to' we read 'Student, Languages', and under 'Religious Denomination' he is 'Church of England'. In fact, the Webbs belonged to the Church in Wales, though there is no evidence that they were especially devout, and their son's religious convictions have been a private matter for the most part. He has not written about them.

After training at HMS *Collingwood* and HMS *Victory*

he served in a number of ships: the *Nile*, the *Hannibal*, the *Pembroke*, the *Duke*, the *Tetcott*, the *Demetrius* and the *Warren*. He was called up as Ordinary Seaman, and became Able Seaman, Writer, Leading Writer, and, eventually, Petty Officer. The Navy was not swift to recognize his remarkable linguistic abilities, and for two years he served, as it were, 'before the mast'. But in May 1945 he was selected for 'special service' in HMS *Nile*, the base ship in Alexandria, and in October of that year he joined HMS *Hannibal*, the base ship at Trieste. He appears to have been involved in intelligence, interpreting and liaison work, and, by his own account, he worked with the French, Italian, Yugoslav and American navies, and was at one time on the staff of the British Naval Mission to the French Provisional Government. He tells how he was aboard the last ship out of Tobruk before it fell to Rommel's army, and remembers that his nerves were affected by the pounding of the guns in the ships in which he served. He was 'Released in Class A' on 17 August, 1946, and (although this is not stated in his Certificate of Service) his demobilization took place at Largs, in Ayrshire, a remote base on the west coast of Scotland.

So the sailor comes ashore, in a strange place, far from anywhere which he might still call home, at the age of twenty-five, alone, having his half-forgotten working-class background in industrial south Wales, his grammar school achievements and the values they instilled, his Oxford degree in Modern Languages, his recent and vividly remembered wartime experiences, and no visible means of support. He is not, at this time, strongly conscious of his Welsh nationality, and he seems to have had very little in the way of political convictions of any kind. Although he was fluent in several European languages his knowledge of Welsh was rudimentary and unexercised. He had not studied that language at school, and, apart from the few family homes where he heard it spoken, his only real exposure to it would have been at Eisteddfodau, some of which had made an impression on him from early childhood. In an unpublished memoir, 'Atgofion Eisteddfodol', he recalls his initiation:

My first, traumatic experience of an Eisteddfod was at Swansea in 1926 before I was 6 years old but clearly recollected because it was so frightening . . .The shed-like main pavillion was in Victoria Park, almost at the end of our street where the Guild Hall now stands and I was held up to watch Lloyd George orating, glimpsed through the part-open doors. My recollection is of a remote figure with the famous white hair, waving his arms about and very excited, speaking of course, in a language which we did not understand . . . But the real horror was the Gorsedd procession, held at Singleton Park. The wrinkled evil faces of the bards, emphasised by their hideous head-dress, were truly frightening, and as this senile procession shambled past, terror entered my soul and I had to be removed in tears.

It was an unpropitious start, and he pursued a complex love–hate relationship with the Eisteddfod in subsequent decades, though love predominated in later years. He seems to have become convinced of the cultural and political importance of the annual event, while remaining deeply sceptical about much of the flummery, and moderately disapproving of some of the goings-on. He writes:

Its search for non-traditional venues led the Eisteddfod to Flint in 1969, an utterly unsuitable choice. The year of the Investiture, police aggro at its height with some ugly scenes and of course the open-air gymanfa *disintegrated ingloriously between police harassment and the barracking of the Scowsified Deeside scum.*

He disapproved because, by this time, he cared. He attended the Eisteddfod regularly, despite the vagaries of his political views and allegiances. But he drew the line at Haverfordwest in 1972, and did not go:

My attendance had been so regular since 1950 that my absence began a rumour that I had committed suicide.

His increasing absorption with the Eisteddfod in the post-war years is one indication of Harri Webb's journey of discovery back to the Welsh-speaking Wales he had glimpsed and half-heard in the Waunarlwydd of his childhood.

But there were no such adventurous paths available to him when he disembarked at Largs in 1946. The world lay all before him, but he had no place to go, and the next twelve months may well have been one of the most depressed and impotent periods of his life. He spent his time, aimless and demoralized, wandering about in Scotland, not so much on holiday as desolately unemployed. Yet it was here, and at this time, that he discovered and read the work of Hugh MacDiarmid, who was to be one of the major influences on his career. MacDiarmid had been born Christopher Grieve, in 1892 in the 'muckle toon' of Langholm in the Scottish border country. He was a generation older than Harri Webb, and by 1946 he had produced a formidable body of published poetry, beginning with ANNALS OF THE FIVE SENSES, in 1923, and including the 'Hymns to Lenin', 'On a

Raised Beach', and – probably his best known and most influential poem – 'A Drunk Man Looks at the Thistle' (1926). Much of MacDiarmid's poetry was written in a synthetic Scots language, re-created out of lexicography for the occasion, and his personal life was romantic, dedicated and fiercely controversial. This was the man who, after the failure of his career and of his first marriage, had fled to one of the remotest of the Shetland islands, and lived in utter penury and total discomfort in order to write the poems, the mass of poems, which had made his name known and discussed throughout the nation. His son, Michael Grieve, described it:

Wind-blasted Whalsay, sodden with the peat of forgotten centuries where trees grew and none now stand, was home – a bucket or two of earth in the chilled lapping bitterness of the North Sea . . . it was here, in a fisherman's cottage, abandoned because of death, with the net-mending loft steep-staired above, that he sat – a self-induced Scottish Siberia that allowed no compromise, where mind over matter was the reality, the only salvation; and the loneliness of hardship was contrasted by the bubbling fleshpots of success, where ambition spurred by acclamation turned into reputation and recognition.

In the blinding light of hindsight it is easy to see the parallels between Harri Webb and Hugh MacDiarmid. Each has been (to say the least) on the left side of the political spectrum; each has moved restlessly from one party to another; each has been a fearlessly controversial public figure; each has been fiercely patriotic, and deeply concerned with the problems and fascinations of language. Perhaps above all, each has identified himself with the *gwerin*, the ordinary people of his country, and written about them and for them. MacDiarmid, in the 'Second Hymn to Lenin', asks:

> Are my poems spoken in the factories and fields,
>   In the streets o' the toon?
> Gin they're no, then I'm falin' to dae
>   What I ocht to ha' dune.

Harri Webb praises the un-named sons of Great Owain, who will *show the proud Sais what we mean*:

> So here's to the sons of the gwerin
> Who care not for prince or for queen,
> Who'll haul down the red, white and blue, lads,
> And hoist up the red, white and green.

But the value of MacDiarmid to Harri Webb's development may well have been more subtle. The two men did not meet face to face until 1974 in Lampeter, but the reputation of MacDiarmid as a political radical and nationalist, a controversialist, an angry Scot, probably attracted Harri Webb's interest, and suggested a model to be imitated. MacDiarmid 'stood for Scotland' in a special way, and the only parallel in Wales must have been Saunders Lewis, though Lewis wrote exclusively in Welsh. Perhaps Harri Webb caught a vision of himself as the radical representative of English-speaking Wales, and modelled himself, in his early work, on the image so successfully established for Scotland by MacDiarmid.

The summer of 1946 was crucial in Harri Webb's life. It was a time of indecision and depression. He had no idea of what to do with himself or where to go. Demobilized, he had no profession, no job, no ambition, no desire. He had fought in war for 'Great

Britain' or 'the Allies' against a tyranny and an evil he found it easy to detest. He was less convinced of the indissoluble loveliness of the United Kingdom: he was interested in Ireland, he found himself fascinated by Scotland, he knew himself to be Welsh. We are fortunate in that, among his diaries, he has preserved a long, detailed and highly introspective manuscript account of his state of mind in these seminal, formative weeks. The manuscript seems to have been written between about 11 and 19 August, 1946, when he was on a brief visit to the family home in Swansea, and it relates to a period which began with his arrival in Scotland in the autumn of the previous year. His moods swung from elation to depression:

I have never been so happy in the Navy . . . The formula was simple – A roomful of pretty girls to spend the working day with, a mess of boon companions to spend the evenings. Willing hands on all sides for dalliance or drinking . . . And there was Scotland. I fell for Scotland long before I knew what it would mean to me . . . but still had no inkling of those nine months on the Ayrshire coast that have only just ended and whose scenes and atmosphere I do not want to forget.

Those 3 days before my Highland tour started had been full of the most bitter gloom, a sort of nervous intensity emanating from the sodden wreck of a summer, that even now, six weeks later, has not begun . . . I had written straight off, one poem, one evening sitting with my back resting against Cuchulain's grave by the shores of Loch Nell . . . The stay on Iona itself was spoilt by the worry over money – one perfectly good evening wasted waiting for a phone call that never came. There was so much like that.

The longest, and most important entry relates to an experience which, as we can confirm from his diary, took place on the evening of 29 June. It had been a wet and gloomy day:

But when at last the rain had gradually worn itself out, the chief thing to do seemed to be – escape. I walked down the Skelmorlie mile in a drying light. Where the measured milepost stands on a protruding piece of foreshore just before Skelmorlie burn is bridged, I turned off the road and walked along the foreshore . . . the sand was fairly wide here, and the entry of Skelmorlie burn into the sea was prolonged by a curving spit of pebbles that ran like a natural breakwater parallel with the shore . . . and at its tip something in the strange drying light, gleamed bright red. I would walk up to it, across the seapocked turf, along the narrowing pebble spit . . . I was able to be apart from the land, surrounded on three sides by water – by the creeping sea, by the racing burn and by the meeting of both confusedly. The red object was a child's cart, brightly painted, on green wheels with a green shaft – solid and new . . . I chucked an old box into the placid reach of a pool faintly stirred by the spate of Skelmorlie water and propelled it to a more dangerous channel and finally out to sea . . . the same happened to the little cart. There seemed to be nothing else to do with it . . .

The fourth horizon, as I sat watching, the one that bound me to the land, as I sat a little out from it, a little apart among waters, was the outline of the heaped pebble ridge . . . Now, over Arran, the evening was at its best: the great island extended its rugged mass along the firth clear in every detail of its mountainous profile, from the rocky coast north of Goatfell, over the recumbent form of the Sleeping Warrior sharply up to the great challenge of Goatfell itself . . . and somehow, looking at the arrogance of Goatfell . . . [I] felt an answering arrogance leap around my head like a halo of lightning . . .

It reminds him of an experience on the Island of Arran which must have taken place two or three weeks earlier:

On the hills, above Lamlash, above human society . . . had come the answer. Not on the horned altar itself, the granite forehead of frowning storm, invoker of rain . . . but on a lesser height had I seen more clearly, from less than a thousand feet up had I taken afresh the measure of the universe . . . I had in this stupendous scenery carefully immunized myself against the attacks of meaningless Wordsworthian mysticism.

This experience, recollected in the tranquillity of Skelmorlie beach, begets a new and transforming insight:

I sat and considered the fourth horizon and beyond it the rest of the Clyde . . . I detected, as soon as it happened, without introspection or surmise, but with immediacy and excitement that I was looking forward to next winter . . . *This was the first breath of the new life of freedom. And too of reality . . . Those sudden cries of joy that we had vented on occasion had been attempts at what this moment really was, the unsought, incongruous discovery that once again, life was good.*

He made no vows, nor did he give any bond that he 'should be, else sinning greatly, a dedicated Spirit' (Wordsworth, THE PRELUDE, IV. 343–4). Indeed, he is aware of the peril and specifically immunized himself against it. But, recollecting it in the tranquillity of Swansea, some six weeks later, he sees it as a turning-point in his life, and as some sort of spiritual experience which guaranteed and underwrote his decision to do something with his life. It may be that the event on Skelmorlie beach, together with his discovery of MacDiarmid's poetry and *persona*, directed his mind towards a return to live in Wales, and to the life of a writer.

It certainly did not kindle in him any passion to follow in Wordsworth's footsteps and write a great epic poem. He may have written a handful of poems before this time, but the greater part of his writing had been prose, and nothing more than the prose of these vast, voluminous and variegated diaries which he had kept, sometimes assiduously, sometimes neglectfully, for the fifteen years since his schooldays. Of all the hundreds of thousands of words his pen had committed to paper not one had seen the light of day in cold print. At the age of twenty-six he had published nothing.

II

Harri Webb returned to Wales in 1946. He took a course in administration at the technical college in Swansea, and with a growing Welsh consciousness and his 'gift for languages' he learnt Welsh in three months with Professor Ernest Hughes at the University College and with the Reverend R. S. Rogers, editor of *Seren Gomer*. His first employment had nothing to do with literature. He found a job at the offices of Lionite, manufacturers of jewellery cases in Cardiff docks, and lived in various lodgings in Cardiff. It did not last long. He drifted from job to job. He worked as a sales representative in south Wales and in the north of England; he was a grocer's clerk, but got dismissed for inefficiency; he worked for a few months as commissionaire at the Capitol Cinema in Queen Street, Cardiff, and, in his leisure time, he joined the Cardiff Unity Theatre. Strangely, it is the question of a National Theatre for Wales which is the subject of Harri Webb's début as a writer, in a letter to Keidrych Rhys, written from 209 City Road, Cardiff, and published in Rhys's magazine *Wales* (vol. viii. no. 29) in May, 1948. *A Welsh theatre is necessary to reveal us to ourselves*, he writes, and, in a prolepsis of his later polemic style, he cries:

Why, for instance, should the Mid-Rhondda Unity Group be doing JUNO AND THE PAYCOCK? *Why should the Arts Council with whatever good intentions have the field to itself with its subsidised company peddling Priestley in those quaint places whose names they probably can't pronounce? The situation as it stands is a national DISGRACE. And the remedy is so eminently practicable, so sweetly possible . . .*

He lacked confidence in his persuasive powers. He writes:

This letter is too long, too discursive and ill-planned for you to publish, but I would be very pleased to hear from you personally, if you do not consider this too presumptuous a request.

It was not too presumptuous: Rhys published it, and took a later opportunity to meet the writer. From the beginning of their friendship Harri Webb was a great admirer of Keidrych Rhys, and there can be no doubt that it was Rhys who launched him – as he launched so many others – into his career as a writer in and of Wales. Probably, it was Rhys's influence which caused Harri Webb to nail his red, white and green colours to the mast and make his first political gesture when he joined Plaid Cymru in 1948. Ironically, he joined on 23 April – Saint George's Day.

In 1949 he moved to Carmarthen, where he was employed by Keidrych Rhys at the Druid Press in Lammas Street. Two of his poems appeared in WALES (No.31, October, 1949): 'Triumphal Entry' and 'Anial Dir'. These are his first published words as a poet; they are about the landscapes of Wales; they are not very good.

What he read at the Druid Press was far more important than what he wrote. In his own note on 'The Welsh Republican Movement' written in January, 1949, Harri Webb says:

When I went to work with Keidrych Rhys there was a pamphlet lying about the office called 'The Welsh Republic' by C. Bere. But there was so much lying about the office, the accumulated visions of every visionary who had ever envisaged a new Wales, a Wales run by Christianity, electricity, or British Israel . . . Among this great choir, which was visible at first glance only as a drift of untidy papers, the sensible and unsensational voice of the Welsh Republic seemed too calm, too academic to attract much notice, in its brown cover.

Cliff Bere's THE WELSH REPUBLIC appeared in two editions, neither of which is dated. The first is priced at 2*d.*, the second at 3*d.*, and it included the Welsh Republican Manifesto drafted by Ithel Davies. In style it is sober, in its assertions it is stark:

It is certain that the only system of government consistent with the political temper and tradition of the Welsh people is republicanism, and the English crown is an institution which is in all respects alien to Wales. (p.3)

Bere gives precedence to a policy of increasing food production, and advocates de-industrialization and de-militarization. He argues that:

The foundation of Wales's new economy must be a vigorous land re-settlement policy in order to develop and re-populate the neglected lands and highlands of Wales and relieve the excess burden of population and industrialism in the southern valleys. (p.5)

Harri Webb read it, and it influenced his political thinking. But so, too, did the ideas of the other Welsh Republicans he met at this time. He was certainly swiftly disenchanted by the tameness of Plaid Cymru. He writes of

21

. . . that trip to Caerphilly Castle, with Roy Lewis and his harem of flatfooted schoolmarms – my sole activity during my Cardiff membership of the Blaid.

In a long manuscript note (*circa* 7,000 words) which he wrote in January, 1949, he traces the beginnings of his activity as a Republican. About his new friends and colleagues in the movement he is both perceptive and enthusiastic. Ithel Davies, who *has come to be regarded as the leader of the movement*, clearly puzzled him:

Obviously a public man. A barrister. As a speaker: incisive but not convincing and monotonously loud, voice occasionally squeaks on the top notes. A North-Mid-Walian . . . outrageously egocentric . . . but this is hardly enough to account for the man as we have him . . . Ithel is best accepted as he is. I think we all like him.

Tom Williams and his wife Joyce (who subsequently made a reputation as the poet Joyce Herbert) are less enigmatic. Tom is *tough, rather rugged. A long North Wales face, a fierce moustache. Takes a bit of getting to know.* His wife Joyce complements him:

. . . a very refreshing personality to the point of being too much so. Almost a caricature of the virtues of South Welsh . . . She has been described as a blaggard, a fishwife and a disgrace – in her public appearances. She writes as she talks and, I should say has no finesse and neither of her feet on the ground . . . Perhaps altogether she is too much fun. But a movement even like ours needs some effervescence, and with Joyce we will get plenty.

Strangely, he has little to say about Huw Davies, who edited THE WELSH REPUBLICAN, and with whom he worked closely and obviously liked. In the Swansea area there is Haydn Jones (who later became the son-in-law of Saunders Lewis),

the little man with the big jaw, the big voice and the pipe . . .
a man of moods which sometimes remove him from active
circulation . . . He doesn't really seem to have much capacity for
original thought – action is his line – selling, heckling, driving,
shouting.

This is a peculiarly ungenerous judgement of a man
who both then, and in later years, was particularly
generous and hospitable to him. Further north,
farming three farms at Llanarth while writing a
thesis for Idris Foster on the position of women in
medieval Welsh law, is the powerful, slightly sinister
figure of John Legonna:

. . . the Celtic synthesis of Cardigan and Cornwall, whose odd,
challenging name (né Brooks, disappointingly) I have known
since Oxford, when he was a firebrand, a protégé of Rouse's
[sic], a Cornish nationalist, and a name whose writings I have
found as invigorating as they are rebarbative, in University
magazines where they stuck out like Celtic rock among the
decadent rococo of elegant Oxonianism . . . Legonna, it seems,
is strong meat.

Another group he distinguishes as the 'movement
builders', and first among them is Gwilym Prys Dafis
(now Lord Prys-Davies, and Opposition Spokesman
on Northern Ireland), at Aberystwyth:

. . . the most impressive thing about Gwilym was the way other
people talked about him, especially his fellow students. Those
who came down from Aber with him believed in him implicitly
and referred to him in terms which are rare on the mouths of
undergraduates describing their contemporaries . . . I have never
heard him speak in public but I have Huw's word that he has
done very well: once at Tregaron, at a Blaid protest meeting, he

completely put Gwynfor Evans in the shade, which is quite something . . . he has impressed or shocked hearers (according to their Welshness or otherwise) with his fire and eloquence. Added to this, there is his solid ability, his constructive and fearless plans, constitutions and other proposals . . . they seem to me to be the best sort of thing of their kind which we as a movement could possibly have. The constitution of the WRM is entirely his work . . . Gwilym himself is in very delicate health, that he is doomed to a Thomas Davis-like fate, – to die young in the cause of Wales. He has sufficiently impressed Sean MacBride to be given an invitation to recuperate at his expense in the Irish sanatoriums . . . He is perhaps the most fierce Welsh Republican of us all.

Not often has Harri Webb – in private or in public – written so glowingly of anyone. He is complimentary, too, about the Bangor branch of the movement, *largely the creation of two dissimilar but complementary characters: Ifor Huws Wilks* [now a Professor in an American university] *and Peter* [later Pedr] *Lewis.*

Wilks is the perfect ex-officer type, safe, middleclass, North Welsh, studying philosophy, creating an atmosphere of perfect normality and confidence around the outrageous propositions of Republicanism. Pedr is almost odd: gauche, tongue-tied, aggressive, proletarian, a runaway to sea, Coleg Harlech, sent down from Bangor and now chopping at trees. Between them they are perfect: a team with complete mastery of the ball.

Coming south again, he is less impressed by Dr Ceinwen Thomas, whom he believed to have been a leaker of information, but he applauds the solid worth and work of Cliff Bere and Huw Davies. Huw's efforts to keep them all *in constant everyday contact so that a Welsh Republican atmosphere would be created* and Cliff, *with that tenacity and iron will of his,* were obviously important organizers. When the

24

group burned a Union Jack at Blackwood it was Cliff
– *his eyes were almost glazed with rapture, his face tense
with fulfilment* – who drew the most appreciative
verdict:

*From that evening on, that mild summer evening of clear
revealing light, I have put up with all the wet Liberal heresy I
have heard from Cliff because fundamentally I know he's
tougher and more fanatical than any of us . . . It will take more
than the English Empire to pull down Cliff Bere.*

Harri Webb's picture of the Republicans is neither
dispassionate nor objective, and not all would share
it. The historian Alan Butt Philip records that

*The Welsh Republican movement grew out of Plaid Cymru in
the late 1940s, the product of frustration among some party
members (especially students in the University College of Wales,
Aberystwyth) with the tameness and lack of urgency in the
party's leadership.*

He adds:

*The republican movement was never strong in Wales. At its
peak it probably had no more than a hundred members. It was
essentially a movement run by a handful of individuals –
Gwilym Prys Davies, Cliff Bere, Huw Davies, Ithel Davies, and
Harri Webb* (THE WELSH QUESTION, UWP, 1975, 261–3).

But what a handful they were, and what a difference
they made to the rather placid political presence of
the Plaid at that time. Their noisy, opinionated,
utopian vision is publicly preserved in the yellowing
pages of their organ, THE WELSH REPUBLICAN, a bi-
monthly broadsheet which ran for nearly forty issues
between August 1950 and May 1957. Soon after it
was launched Harri Webb was appointed editor, and,

25

indeed he wrote a large part of most issues, either under his own name or under pseudonyms or anonymously. It is in THE WELSH REPUBLICAN that Harri Webb emerges as a journalist, a political commentator, essayist, opinion-former and campaigner: in short, as one of the Writers of Wales.

The early issues of THE WELSH REPUBLICAN (*Y Gwerinaethwr*) are full of fight, fire and optimism. Glyn Thomas thunders against the threat of closure at Cilely pit, and Tom Williams writes on 'Our attitude to England's Wars' (Vol. I No. 2, Oct.–Nov. 1950), and the following number features Ithel Davies's 'Hands Off Our Homes: Abolish Leaseholds'. Harri Webb contributes an unambiguous editorial beginning: *The year 1950, the first full year of organised Welsh Republican campaigning, has been a success.* The evidence he adduces in support of this claim includes the fact that a Welsh Republican stood for the first time as a candidate in a General Election to England's Parliament, that representatives were sent to an Easter demonstration of Celtic solidarity in Dun Laoghaire, Dublin, and that the spring and summer had seen speakers on street-corners and in the squares of every township between Carmarthen and Gwent. There had been open-air meetings at which the Union Jack had been burned, and four Republicans had been charged with endangering public order and fined. There had been attacks on the Union Jack (which the editor describes graphically) at the Caerffili Eisteddfod, as a result of which two more fines had been extracted from Republicans. For an editor, these are thin pickings; he did not have much upon which to rejoice, but the tone is resolutely triumphant, as it was to be throughout the newspaper's life. Typical of Harri Webb's campaign-

26

ing style is his report in the same issue (Vol. I No. 3, Dec. 50–Jan. 51) on the Welsh White Paper 'The Government Report on Action in Wales for 1950':

. . . it is the smug self-justification of those gents whose labours require the use of so many acres of air-conditioned, plush-lined office space in the centre of Cardiff to maintain themselves in the privileged purlieus of Penarth and Penylan.

Many another hack might have managed the adjectives and the alliteration; the neat placing of the diminutive 'gents' marks this as Harri Webb's.

The paper raises serious issues and argues them seriously. Vol I No. 4 (Feb.–March 1951) features Dr D. J. Davies on 'Steel – The Truth. The Meaning of Margam', Jac L. Williams on 'The National', and John Legonna on 'Wales and the World'. Harri Webb contributes a signed article 'We believe in the Welsh People: The Basis of our Action', and his editorial is on the Committee of the Parliament for Wales campaign:

It would be a grave error to believe either in the wording or the efficacy of the Committee's Petition . . .

Two years later the paper champions the cause of Gwyndaf Evans and Peter Lewis (subsequently known as Pedr Lewis), the two young men arrested on explosives charges. 'Police Pounce on Patriots' is the headline (Vol. 3 No. 5, April–May). Pedr Lewis was found guilty of possessing two hundred detonators and sentenced to eighteen months in prison, during which time the paper regularly reminded its readers of his plight, and gave full coverage of the dinner in his honour which celebrated his eventual release. Yet in that same issue of April–May, 1953 Harri Webb's editorial was general rather than particular. He lamented

. . . the abandonment by the Labour Party of a Welsh Home Rule Policy . . . and the hesitancy and general middle-class inadequacy of the established Nationalist organisation, Plaid Cymru.

In Vol. V No. 1 (Aug.–Sept., 1954) Gwilym Prys Dafis (later the Labour peer Lord Prys-Davies) contributed a chillingly factual account of the depopulation of rural Wales, entitled 'Rural Wales: The Way Ahead. Challenge to Apathy', and as late as 1957 the paper was campaigning over the danger to the Tryweryn Valley from the Liverpool reservoir scheme. There were many issues which Welsh Republicanism did not address, but it did, eventually, take an interest in the question of just where the borders of the Welsh Republic should be. In two consecutive issues in 1957 'Manawyd' (i.e. Harri Webb) argued for the historical Dee–Severn line first proposed by Owain Glyndŵr, and supported this claim with a wealth of persuasive detail. And, of course, the paper had its heroes on the contemporary scene, chief of whom was S. O. Davies, MP for Merthyr, who presented 'A Bill for the Better Government of Wales' to the Commons. Harri Webb praised him (Vol. 5 No. 4, Feb.–March 1955) as *a true Socialist who can neither be bullied nor bought*. Clearly, here was a man for whom Harri Webb had high hopes, and they are in line with his general political thinking. As early as the sixth issue he had declared his inheritance:

So Welsh Republicanism develops as the practical successor to English Labour 'socialism'.

The idea of the Welsh Republicans as 'practical' in any serious political sense might raise the odd eyebrow today. But things were different then.

There was wit, and satire, and comedy and laughter in THE WELSH REPUBLICAN. The early issues contained a regular column by 'Spy' (Harri Webb) called 'Guilty Men', a hilariously scurrilous series of attacks on the good and the great of Welsh society. The targets included the Marquess of Anglesey, Gwilym Lloyd George, Major Tasker Watkins VC (who got off comparatively lightly), Megan Lloyd George (who didn't), Captain Roderic Bowen and Lord Lloyd of Dolobran. 'Spy' and his column disappeared after a while, probably because the threat of libel suits to such an impecunious newspaper was too perilous. The best, and the most daring, was probably No. 3 on 'Dr Thomas Jones, CH', which began: *Before the career of Thomas Jones, criticism is respectfully dumb.*

Two of Harri Webb's poems were first published in THE WELSH REPUBLICAN. In the Oct.–Nov. issue of 1955, over the pseudonym 'Gŵyrfab' appeared 'The Disclaimers', a poem about the daring Scots reclaiming the Stone of Scone, and the next issue printed (in a version slightly different from the later one in THE GREEN DESERT, reproduced here) his 'Epitaph for a Great Welshman':

> *Where now he lies his old routine*
> *Will suffer scant disruption*
> *For none could say he'd ever been*
> *A stranger to corruption.*

A small thing, but not unworthy, and typical of Webb's tone as both editor and contributor.

In the Feb.–March 1955 issue (Vol. 5, No. 4) Harri Webb includes a quite extensive comic extravaganza entitled 'The Babes in Milk Wood: an Interlude', in the style of a pantomime. Villainous (English) villains stalk the stage, and young Dai (the simple hero) is in many and great dangers until the appearance of the Fairy Megan (daughter of David Lloyd George), who announces:

> *The bounteous Fairy Megan, I*
> *And I will help you all I can.*
> *Dai (aside): We heard the same from your old man.*

THE WELSH REPUBLICAN, under Harri Webb's editorship, may have been tendentious, may have been alarming, but it was not dull. The last issue was for April–May 1957, and it contains no hint that the paper was closing down. It just stopped.

Both as writer and as editor (for he collected some able and talented contributors for the paper) Harri Webb did much to define the concerns and policies of Welsh Republicanism in the 1950s. In one article after another he explained the Republican interpretation of Welsh history, he orchestrated the publicity for their campaigns, and he presented the flag-burning episodes as heroic acts of patriotic defiance by a gallant commando of freedom-fighters, when to many in Wales, especially the constabulary, they hardly seemed to be quite that. Above all, THE WELSH REPUBLICAN made a refreshing contrast to the more sober-sided, polite publication of Plaid Cymru, WELSH NATION. For seven years Harri Webb attracted a reasonably substantial number of people, particularly in south-east Wales, to see that nationalist politics could be convivial, congenial, exciting, even slightly glorious. His achievement is that he presented The Revolution as fun.

If the newspaper was, for seven years, a lively and regular institution, Harri Webb's personal life at this time was unhappy, unsettled, unsuccessful, and nomadic. In 1949 he left Carmarthen and returned to Swansea, left Swansea and moved to Cardiff, where he worked for the Principality Educational Depot, booksellers, at a salary of £5. 6s. a week until he was made redundant. In 1951 he joined Cliff Bere and Huw Dafis in running a bookshop in Bargoed, and lived there at 104 Gilfach Street. The business venture failed, of course. He was briefly employed with the Ford Motor Company. In the following year he worked for a few months in a bookshop at Malvern, but throughout these years he was in poor health and decidedly impecunious. Things began slowly to improve when he landed a job in Cheltenham Public Library in 1952, and stayed there for nearly two years at a salary of £425 a year. He lived at Whistling Down Hay, Cleeve Hill, the home of Ben and Barbara Howard, Anglo-Irish bohemians and publishers of the little magazine *Promenade*, to which he contributed. What was probably his last 'public appearance' on behalf of the Welsh Republican movement took place on Sunday, 5 October, 1952. He addressed a public meeting in Trafalgar Square, in company with three other speakers; they are listed on the flysheet as *Wendy Wood, Meredith Edwards (Plaid Cymru), Harry Webb (Welsh Republic) and Sean Caernoig (Sinn Fein Ireland)*. In the following year he joined the Labour Party, and his membership cards survive for the period 1953–8. He left the Labour Party in 1958 and rejoined Plaid Cymru two years later.

His experience at Cheltenham Public Library stood him in good stead, since, in 1954, he was appointed librarian in charge of the Dowlais branch library in Merthyr Tydfil. He moved to Merthyr and lived there in more or less settled circumstances. He became active with the local Labour Party, and developed a strong interest in the culture and history of the town. He has retained this interest all his life. What may be his last poem (PLANET, Aug.–Sept. 1989) is a sonnet called 'Dowlais':

> That lift of wonder in the Lusiads
> When all the marvels of the eastern sea
> Sparkled and shone in endless mystery
> To daze the hungry eyes of Vasco's lads
> With scenes undreamt of, isles of luxury,
> Promises of pleasure, loot and mastery,
> Empire unheard of, opulent dowry,
> Indies on Indies dazzling myriads,
> Was mine when on an iron January day
> I first saw Dowlais on its iron hill
> And all was iron, like its history,
> The stone, the scowling church, the air
> All gave me welcome and all said
> At last, after long wandering, you're there.

Part of his political activity took the form of lectures to Labour Party audiences. These appear to have been highly successful, and one of them, on Dic Penderyn, was published as a sixteen-page pamphlet in 1956. It was a pioneering study, on which later historians have relied, and it presented a riot as a rising. Harri Webb said later *I never wrote anything of worth before I became a political activist* (ARTISTS IN WALES (3), ed. Meic Stephens, 1977, p.90), and this pamphlet is the first publication to bear his name on the cover. As an account of the Merthyr Rising of

1831 it is an accurate and well-ordered narrative, which the researches of subsequent historians have done little to modify or correct. But the tone is neither impartial nor appraising. There is no doubt whose side the author is on; and Dic Penderyn emerges as one of Merthyr's martyrs every bit as important as its eponymous virgin. Its opening is characteristic:

Merthyr Tydfil in 1831 – the industrial centre of gravity of the universe – the greatest populated place in Wales, larger than Cardiff and Swansea and Newport put together – the satanic metropolis of iron, built in the image of the ironmasters, where the flaring furnaces cast their lurid light on the gleaming new stonework of Cyfarthfa Castle, and over the unspeakable slum homes of the workers.

He relates the events of 'Bloody Friday' with dramatic panache:

The bold, masterful Crawshay impatiently strode forward in his eagerness to speak his mind to his men. 'Villains!' he blared, and proceeded to abuse and insult them.

And so it goes on. *The house was full of soldiers whose bayonets had already drunk Welsh blood*, he writes, and at the end

the masters reined in their fine horses . . . looked over the fair land they had looted and raped and defiled, and then cantered off downhill to a good lunch, well satisfied.

Even the account of Dic's hanging includes thunder and lightning, and the crowd sinking to their knees:

The storm raged and the thunder rolled as the artillery of Heaven itself saluted the passing of a chieftain.

33

But the final great comparison is reserved for the final scene:

Dic Penderyn received Christian burial in the graveyard of St Mary's Church, and the Mother of God took into her keeping the son of another mother who, like her own, had met his death at the hands of evil men for the great love he bore his people.

It is easy to smile, and murmur 'a touch over the top, perhaps', but the writing in this pamphlet is remarkably revealing about Harri Webb's style on political subjects. It is rhetorical, theatrical, highly coloured, and often lurid, but it is self-consciously so. For the purposes of his polemic Crawshay must be painted like the villain of a Victorian melodrama, Dic's death may legitimately be compared to Christ's, because in Harri Webb's political pronouncements there is no compromise, everything is jet-black or snow-white. His writing is confrontational, adversarial, and his account of the Merthyr Rising is unashamedly a florid and forensic discourse for the defence, which is engaging and persuasive precisely because it is so close to comic exaggeration.

The following years, indeed all the rest of the 1950s, were comparatively uneventful and, from a literary point of view an unproductive period. His father's death in 1956 severed the last, vestigial link with his family in Swansea, and apart from unsuccessful applications for the post of Keeper of Printed Books at the National Library of Wales and a post in Perth, Australia, he seems to have been content to settle down in Merthyr Tydfil and develop his work as librarian. It is notable that he has never needed nor acquired any professional qualifications in librarianship or information science; this has in no way prevented him from being an extremely effective librarian.

He was still a regular Eisteddfodwr, and his notes record his satisfaction with the Eisteddfod of 1956:

The venue was Aberdare Park, and there has been a general and abiding consensus that this was one of the best Eisteddfodau ever.

He was less impressed at Cardiff in 1960:

. . . uncomfortably beset by controversy – which belongs, I'm sure, to history. There was, as usual in Cardiff, no chairing, and the whole thing was pretty di-fflach [lifeless], *as was the atmosphere in the community at large . . . The Plaid Cymru conference was something else again, held on the Colchester Avenue Campus and my first* official *attendance – and quite an eye-opener. Ever tolerant in such matters, I still found it difficult to credit the open lechery as the gilded flies went to it. On Sunday there they all were in Capel Heol y Crwys, demure under their* gymanfa [singing festival] *hats. It was the year of Fellini's* LA DOLCE VITA.

He had left the Labour Party in 1958, and rejoined the Plaid at the 1960 Summer School in Machynlleth. In the same year he moved into Garth Newydd, a large house on the Brecon Road in Merthyr, previously (ironically) a Victorian iron-master's house. The story of Garth Newydd, and Harri Webb's various co-tenants, the suspicions of the police that the place was the headquarters of Radio Free Wales, and the endless discussions of literature and politics over mountains of (mostly fried) food, has been told by Meic Stephens in PLANET, 83 (1990). Harri Webb and Meic Stephens first met in the summer of 1962, and their friendship was instant. They had a lot in common. Both came from industrial, English-speaking Wales; both their fathers had spent their working lives in electric power stations; both had degrees in Romance languages; they agreed about literature and politics, and shared an admiration for poets like Lorca, Prévert, Neruda, Eluard and MacDiarmid.

Meic Stephens moved into Garth Newydd in the late summer of 1962, and others soon joined them there: Judy Gurney, Tony Lewis, Neil Jenkins, Rodric Evans, Dave Buckel and Peter Meazey were the principal residents, but many others came, for shorter or longer periods, and went. As Meic Stephens wrote:

The cause that bound us together was that of Plaid Cymru and we were all active on its behalf in Merthyr and neighbouring constituencies. Harri was doing a stint as editor of WELSH NATION, *the party's newspaper, while the rest of us were helping to challenge the dead hand of the Labour Party in 'the rotten borough'.*

The 'stint as editor' was from 1962 to 1964, though Harri Webb had contributed a letter and an article to WELSH NATION as early as 1956. In November 1961 his speech proposing the main motion at Plaid Cymru's annual conference was reported at length, under the title 'The National Integrity of Wales', and it gives a fair flavour of his platform rhetoric together with a foretaste of what was to become one of the insistent images of his poetry:

From Hawarden to Llandudno – or from de Haviland's to Hotpoint; from Newport to Swansea – or from Spencers to Prestcold, some of us have never had it so good. But in between, between Hotpoint and Prestcold, there stretch first, the intermediate zones – the twilight zones of unstable economy and uncertain prospects, and, back of them again, the Green Desert . . .

His experience of the Western desert in wartime may underpin Harri Webb's deployment of the desert image in his poems, but in them, and for him, a desert is a very bad place in which to be.

In May 1962, under the pseudonym Gŵyrfab, which he brought with him from his WELSH REPUBLICAN days, he contributed a gnomic little poem, 'Excelsior':

> *In thirty-six he lit a flame*
> *That lept* [sic] *from hill to hill.*
> *In sixty-two he's just the same;*
> *Burning up rubbish still.*

The allusion, and it is wholly approving, is to Saunders Lewis and the arson at Penyberth: the point is that 'he' is not directly identified (there were at least three people concerned), and that 'thirty-six' would only be meaningful to those who knew the history and were in sympathy with the cause. This indirect, allusive, codified communication (to be seen at its best in 'Song for July' in THE GREEN Desert) is characteristic of Harri Webb both as journalist and poet. The comic columns, 'It's almost news' and 'The Land of Pong' which he contributed sporadically to WELSH NATION under the name of John Spang, are usually constructed on this principle. Sometimes the characters' names are quite spectacularly unfunny: we could do without Mr Catullus Clinker and Mr Dai O'Rheea. Occasionally, an invented name cloaks (for the initiated) an easily recognizable one, as in the issue of April 1963:

The Revd Ben Z. Reen was recently inducted to the joint
pastorates of Sodom and Gomorrah, in Cwmgrafft . . .

What the Reverend D. Ben Rees, the well-known and
respected Nonconformist minister from Llanddewi-
brefi, prominent in the Labour Party, had done to
earn Webb's barbed accolade will never be known,
but these columns struck a new and distinctly sharp
note in a newspaper hitherto characterized by moder-
ation and gentility.

The issue of September 1962 is the first to name
Harri Webb as editor, and J. Gwyn Griffiths takes
over from him in August, 1964. Between these dates
Webb contributes comparatively little under his own
name, and many of his editorials lack lustre:

It is natural, as the year draws to its close, for a mood of
retrospection to set in, re-inforced by the customs of the season
which brings together separated families and friends. (Dec.
1962).

It needs only a reference to the festive board to
complete the rollcall of ringing clichés. It may be that
the onerous office of editor compelled him to con-
form to the blandness of Plaid Cymru, and his polite
and respectful disagreement with Gwilym Prys-
Davies, in the issue of February, 1964, on the best
tactics for achieving self-government, itself achieves
all the solemnity of a requiem mass. Mercifully, there
are other moments when Webb's wit breaks surface,
as when he writes in his tribute to Augustus John in
August 1962:

I have seen a group of Yorkshire colliers stand rivetted in

38

admiration before his drawing of a whippet in the Barnsley Art Gallery . . .

And his quotation of himself in 'Conference Quotes' in September 1963:

Unlike Christine Keeler, we are not going to lie down under the English Government.

His later editorials, however, though they are faithful to the party line, lack fire, and towards the end of his period as editor, he seems close to disillusion. In his editorial of February, 1964 he writes:

If self-government is not achieved within the lifetime of those of us who have not yet reached middle age, then, sometime in the twenty-first century the Welsh nation may well cease to exist. It will not have succumbed for force of arms, nor yet to economic rapine nor to political pressure, weighty though these factors may be. It will have been undermined by its own rotten-ness. It will have gone down because those Welsh people who are alive today were base. It will have died because it did not deserve to live.

When he wrote thus of *those of us who have not yet reached middle age* he was himself forty-three years old.

It may well be that the remembrance of his editorial duties was grievous unto him, and the burden of them was intolerable. It is certain that, when he laid down the office his contributions to Welsh Nation resumed their characteristic style – though there is one exception, a wholly uncharacteristic poem, in the issue for April 1965, which has never been reprinted. It reveals something about Harri Webb which nothing in his other writings would disclose. The title is 'Whose Funeral?'

> They say that he himself prepared
> The order of his going, drew up in detail
> The plans for the state funeral and the simple
> Committal in the earth he loved so well
> In the way of his time and people
> For whom now time ends.
> > It takes a great man
> To think in these terms. He was a good enemy.
> And now his own, in taking leave of him
> Take leave too of all that they once were,
> Not understanding, perhaps, what they are doing
> Or only partly understanding, or perhaps
> Understanding too well.

Winston Churchill was buried, after a most magnificent state funeral, in the simplicity of an Oxfordshire churchyard on 30 January 1965. Perhaps in this odd poem we see one old sailor recognizing another. There is something of this in his later poem on Churchill, 'Butties All' in POEMS AND POINTS.

Harri Webb published several other poems in WELSH NATION which he has chosen not to reprint. Some of them are, in John Donne's phrase, 'light squibs', like 'A ballad of the fourteenth of July', which appeared in September 1966, and begins:

> When Gwynfor got in for Carmarthen
> Old Merlin was roused by our roar . . .

– this incidentally, is the first contribution in which he acknowledges his pseudonym, and signs 'Harri Webb (Gŵyrfab)'. Others are more serious, like 'To the Memory of a Friend' (WELSH NATION), 17 March 1972), his elegy on S. O. Davies, MP.

His prose pieces resume their former campaigning aggressiveness, and his targets are familiar. In January 1969, in the column 'One Man's Wales', he comments on Harold Wilson's recent visit:

> . . . *inside the building the Prime Minister was being assured by his devoted fan, Mr George Thomas, that he was loved by the people of Wales as no politician in history had ever been loved. George is always pretty sickening, but this performance under such circumstances must surely take some beating for macabre irony. It reminds one of the sycophantic chanting of eunuchs at the court of some oriental tyrant. Or the atmosphere in the Führer's bunker.*

He is to be seen at his most violent (again in the 'One Man's Wales' column) in April 1969, the time of the investiture of the Prince of Wales. He notices that the artist who designed the prince's crown had said that the crown had much in common with the crown of thorns worn by Christ on the cross. Webb asks *Why didn't they go the whole hog?* Usually, however, his victims are politicians. In September 1970 he reported Michael Foot's election to the Shadow Cabinet, and says: *Doubtless he will do his best to drag it kicking and screaming into the 17th century.* And two months later he takes a genial sideswipe at one of the leading liberals, *that amiable political coelacanth, Mr Emlyn Hooson.* His rich contempt for all political parties other than the Plaid is evident when he reviews the Party Conferences in October, 1976. He dismisses the Liberals: they are 'exhausted beyond recovery'. He turns to the ruling party:

The Conservatives' Welsh Conference also had its moments, Mrs Thatcher showing her indomitable spirit by valiantly attempting to pronounce a token sentence in yr hen iaith . . .

and then to the Opposition:

. . . there was Neil Kinnock raucously at it, to be followed by Michael Foot, an exponent of the Higher Confusion, who, as far as anyone could follow him at all, appeared to equate devolution with all sorts of goodies that everyone is in favour of.

In December, 1976, he is cheered by the possibility that a devolved Welsh Assembly might be housed in the Coal Exchange building in Cardiff Docks. He finds the prospect fortifying, and he is relieved that the Assembly would not assemble *in the dreadful 'Temple of Peace'* an edifice which moves him to remember Keats:

The building itself is tame and innocuous enough, a sort of petty-bourgeois Parthenon, a pacifist Valhalla, in itself a depressing contrast to the fullblooded baroque of the Coal Exchange, but to call an office block a temple . . . has always screamed to me a bit comic. I wonder what rites are supposed to go on there? What men and gods are these? What maidens loth? What mad pursuit? What struggles to escape? What pipes and timbrels? What wild ecstasy? Well, actually it's the headquarters of the South Glamorgan Health Authority . . .

He was probably on safe ground in assuming that his readers would see the point of the comparison between The Temple of Peace and The Grecian Urn, and might even recall that *Beauty is Truth, Truth Beauty: that is all ye know on earth, and all ye need to know.*

42

III

Webb's contributions to WELSH NATION were substantial, distinguished and continuous over a long period. But they are not the only fruits of his political thinking. Throughout the sixties his sympathies had developed in new directions. Although he maintained his membership of Plaid Cymru he had grown increasingly impatient of its passivity and its quietism, and become more interested in initiatives like the 'New Nation' movement which looked likely to challenge the orthodoxies and achieve tangible political results. 'New Nation' was a pressure-group within Plaid Cymru, seeking radical reform from within. Its programme is announced in its 'Remonstrance' printed in the first issue of its journal CILMERI, in December 1965, and including such statements as:

WE TESTIFY that despite seven centuries of Anglicisation since the fall of Llywelyn, Wales still lives, and we affirm that whatever her divisions Wales is a national entity and shall be intact and inviolate within her true boundaries . . .
WE CALL upon those who already profess allegiance to the national cause by their membership of Plaid Cymru to take the implications of that allegiance more seriously . . . We urge unspairing [sic] self-examination and a strict rendering of account for stewardship, bearing in mind the harsh judgements that history has in store for good intentions not governed by rigorous attention to reality . . .

The Remonstrance is signed 'In the name of New Nation' by Emrys Roberts, Ray Smith, Harri Webb, Roger Boore, and John Legonna. Emrys Roberts (sometime Secretary of the Plaid) seems to have been the prime force in the movement, and a photograph of him laying a wreath at the monument to Llywelyn the Last erected at Cilmeri, Breconshire, close to the ford on the River Irfon, where he was killed in 1282, accompanies Harri Webb's 'Song of Cilmeri', a rhetorical and emotional prose meditation upon the occasion and its modern consequences. He writes:

His death is mean and meaningless in a cause already lost, under squalid and mysterious circumstances of which contradictory versions still circulate. In that, at least, he is one with all the wasted dead of Wales, from Morfa Rhuddlan to Mametz Wood, from the field of Catraeth to the coalface of the Cambrian.

Ray Smith, chairman of 'New Nation', contributed an article on the shortcomings of Plaid Cymru, 'Our Fortieth Year to Failure', in which he says:

If the party can learn that there is no more frequent or more saddening epitaph in the whole of history than, 'We have always done it this way', there is a chance of success. It is this belief that led to the formation of 'New Nation', a group of nationalists who wish to see Plaid Cymru become a Party worthy of its cause.

By contrast to such exhortations, Emrys Roberts argues coldly and cogently for reform of administration within the Plaid, including proposals for the improvement of accounting methods, the introduction of budgetary control, and the modernization of the party's newspapers. 'New Nation' was not a puff of fanciful idealism. It kept at least one foot on the ground. And it took care to open its modest bank account not in Cardiff, but in Dublin.

Harri Webb contributed to CILMERI and to its off-shoot CILMERI CENTREPOINT, with political articles, a poem, a review, but neither the journal nor the movement seem to have survived long after the winter of 1966. Yet Harri Webb laboured on, continuously active behind the scenes, in promulgating and publicizing the crucial issues in the Welsh Nationalist cause, and he was tireless in his concern for detailed accuracy of expression. An (unpublished) letter to Gwilym Prys-Davies, dated 2 October 1965, on the question of an elected Council for Wales with executive responsibilities, illustrates his concerns:

Dear Gwilym,
Despite the Commonwealth Arts Festival and the Library Association conference, I have found time to draft the letter. I enclose a copy spaced for plentiful, and, I am sure, very necessary emendation, and have put in one or two remarks of my own in places where there is some doubt in my mind about points that it may be wiser to leave out at this stage, and then there is the ending which will depend on the views of the signatories who have not yet been canvassed. Obviously a fair amount of circulation of drafts will have to take place before an agreed version can be sent for publication.

All this referred to a letter intended for THE TIMES or The DAILY TELEGRAPH. Indeed, it was a time of great letter-writing. And Harri Webb's contributions were no more than a part of the plethora of correspondence which united the thinkers, the dreamers, the planners, the prophets, the would-be administrators, the poets and the politicians who espoused the nationalist cause. For example, the John Legonna Papers, including the letters which form a substantial bequest in the National Library of Wales, are by no means the complete surviving correspondence of that one nationalist alone: many letters are still in private hands.

The political activity was substantial, but it should not be forgotten that Harri Webb was earning his living as the Librarian of Mountain Ash, and the work was not always tranquil. On 11 December, 1965, the ABERDARE LEADER reported:

Reading Rooms in public libraries are there for the use of all sections of the community including women. That is the answer of Mountain Ash Council's Librarian, Mr Harri Webb MA, who has been criticised for purchasing at 4s. a copy of the glossy women's magazine VOGUE for the reading rooms of the Mountain Ash central and branch libraries.

The fearless investigative reporter further revealed that Mr Webb had incurred the displeasure of Councillor (Miss) E. M. Bath, chairman of the Libraries Committee, by his radical, ruthless and revolutionary idea of his duties:

Mr Webb acted always with the best interests of the library service at heart but in doing so he had annoyed some people. He had discarded some books which were regarded by some as of value. And he had taken pictures down from the walls and taken a valuable bookcase out of one of the libraries and put it in a corridor. 'It has caused a furore at Penrhiwceiber,' she declared.

To have spent some twenty years campaigning in print and at public meetings for an end to English rule, for self-government, for a workers' republic of Wales, for the centrality in Wales of its language and its culture, was one thing: taking a valuable bookcase and putting it in a corridor was something else again.

Harri Webb's political journalism and pamphlet-eering has never been properly assessed or appreciated. No selections from it have been published. Yet until he wrote in such technicolour terms the story of Dic Penderyn and the Merthyr Rising it is no exaggeration to say that the professional historians had almost totally ignored it. Since then, no account of nineteenth-century Welsh history dare leave it out. It was Harri Webb who first asserted the importance of the Welsh national anthem, explained its unusual language and set it in its historical and cultural context. Above all, it was his newspaper journalism, week in, week out, which kept the events, the ideas, the characters of Welsh nationalism perpetually in the public consciousness, and made them interesting, exciting and attractive to the reader. In THE WELSH REPUBLICAN, WELSH NATION, the WESTERN MAIL and elsewhere, for more than thirty years, his writing demanded attention. He had a particular 'praising' gift for confident, positive hyperbole, which could make his account of the attack on the Union Jack at the Caerffili Eisteddfod seem momentarily as important as the fall of Troy. Similarly, when he sums up an argument with the words *So Welsh Republicanism develops as the practical successor to English Labour 'socialism'* there is a tone of invincible incontrovertibility which goes far to persuade the reader that it might, in certain circumstances, even, possibly, be so. The obverse is equally true. As a satirical journalist Harri Webb was properly malicious, endlessly inventive, and deeply destructive. His regular columns – 'It's almost news', 'The Land of Pong', 'One Man's Wales' – ran for long periods without losing their savage bite. His targets were usually pompous people, hypocrites of various kinds (and Wales has seldom been short of them), corrupt practices in local politics, and, above all, Welsh people who ignored, despised or slighted Wales. He wrote about them in a rich, resonant, articulate and highly colourful prose which, at a time when Plaid Cymru was not making headlines, Cymdeithas yr Iaith Gymraeg's 'events' lay all in the future, and the art of arson was in its infancy, stood out in Welsh journalism like a good deed in a naughty world.

It was the coincidence of Meic Stephens and Harri Webb at Garth Newydd, at a time when Webb was settling in as a citizen of the town he described as *that raffish mini-metropolis Merthyr Tydfil, with all its fascinating paradoxes*, that saw the emergence into public view of Harri Webb the poet. He seems to have written poems, unconcernedly, since childhood. He was a student and lover of poetry in several languages, but it was not until he lived in the same house and worked closely with Meic Stephens on political, journalistic and literary matters in the years following 1962 that his poetry achieved a public dimension.

Nearly all Harri Webb's earlier poems had appeared, almost casually, in newspapers. He had seldom sought publication in literary magazines, and the poems he wrote for THE WELSH REPUBLICAN, WEST-ERN MAIL, and WELSH NATION were brief, witty, political, occasional, ephemeral and designed for the particular readership. It was popular, coterie verse. Meic Stephens, on the other hand, had written both serious poems and songs, ballads and satires on contemporary events. He had also developed an interest in publishing and editing poetry. The part-nership between Stephens and Webb in founding the

Triskel Press, a publishing imprint intended to present the work of Welsh writers in English, enabled Harri Webb's poetry to develop a new dimension. Triskel's first publication, in 1963, was a fifty-eight page booklet entitled TRIAD, containing thirty-three poems by Peter Griffith (later known as Peter Gruffydd), Harri Webb and Meic Stephens. As Anthony Conran points out in his Introduction:

What they have in common is the experience of exile: not necessarily physical exile, but exile from the inmost heart of their country. All three of them speak English as their first language . . . All three have turned to political Nationalism as the only thing that offers them, and the generations that will come after them, any hope whatever of avoiding exile that has wounded them.

Conran's sentiments may seem a little portentous now, but they caught the mood of 1963. His début in TRIAD obliged Harri Webb to select poems with which to present himself to a poetry-reading public who might or might not share his political views, but would evaluate him principally as a poet. His selection, and his self-presentation, are testificatory: they are also proleptic, and the key to all his later poetry. He prefaces his selection with two lines of verse:

Er colli'r tir o hirynt
Y tir a geir o try'r gwynt.

They are in Welsh, he does not translate them, he does not ascribe them to any author. They come, in fact, from a *cywydd* by Iorwerth Fynglwyd (*floreat* 1480–1527) to Rhys ap Siôn o Lyn Nedd, and can be found in *Gwaith Iorwerth Fynglwyd* (ed. Howell Ll. Jones and E. J. Rowlands, Cardiff, University of

Wales Press, 1975). Harri Webb may well have found them, however, in Thomas Parry's *Oxford Book of Welsh Verse* (p.196). This first appeared in 1962, a year before the publication of TRIAD.

Not every first-class honours graduate in Welsh would be expected to recognize those lines and know who wrote them. To quote them thus, in the very forehead of his first collection, is Webb's peremptory assertion of his scholarship, his standing, his pretensions and his subject. And the first poem in the collection, 'Big Night', promptly deflates the assertion:

> *We started drinking at seven*
> *And went out for a breather at ten,*
> *And all the stars in heaven*
> *Said: Go back and drink again.*

It is a rollicking account of a night's drinking, Dylanesque, Falstaffian – he has heard the chimes at midnight – alongside the headwaters of the tipsy Taff. It comes first to counter any assumption on the part of the reader that the scholarly Harri Webb cannot also be the drunken Webb; he is large, he contains multitudes. 'Big night' is immediately followed by 'Valley Winter', a wholly serious, powerful poem, which opens with one of his finest images:

> *Under the gaslamps, the wet brown fallen leaves*
> *Glitter like glass of broken beer bottles;*
> *The feast is finished, the hangover remains.*

The alcoholic continuity between the first two poems is in stark contrast to the utterly opposite tones and intentions. The juxtaposition is shrewd, and deliberate. The third poem is the rough-and-tumble comic ballad 'Local Boy Makes Good', its very title a sardonic glance at provincial newspaper cliché, which begins:

> When Christ was born on Dowlais Top
> The ironworks were all on stop.

Set in the *holy land* between Merthyr, Swansea and Cardiff, the targets of this simple satire are *the authorities, the public men on the boards and panels*, the righteous, the respectable, and they are duly mocked. In total contrast, the next poem, 'Triumphal Entry' (one end of Christ's life ironically echoing the other) is a full-bodied poem of praise to the River Taff. No one had thought to do that before: the Taff is not obviously poetic. And so the pattern of surprising contrasts goes on. 'Llys Ifor Hael' is a translation from the Welsh of Ieuan Fardd (1731–88), and it is separated form 'Young Fellow from Lleyn', translated from the Welsh of William Jones (1896–1961), by the tiny lyric 'Towy Idyll', a poem about a coracle. 'Carmarthen Coast' is a consciously 'literary' poem, opening with a line to out-Dylan Dylan:

> Sea-hung cages of singing, hymn-barns . . .

it is wryly appropriate to a description of the coast near Laugharne. The poem continues in T. S. Eliot's voice:

> You must stay
> Or wander back to the parked car
> In the lane that leads nowhere . . .

But the point of the poem, crisply made in its last

two lines, is that none of these styles or voices will do for contemporary Wales, which is neither Llareggub or Little Gidding:

You have brought no prayers, no tears. You must return
To the towns without laughter and the valleys without pride.

The three poems which complete the selection, 'Ty Ddewi', 'The Nightingales', and 'To Wales', are in the same vein. They are serious poems about Wales past and present, and, though the styles are quite different, they share an imperative to action – to sing, in 'The Nightingales',

You have outsung all our dead poets
Sing for them again in Cwm Prysor and Dyffryn Ceiriog . . .

and in the final poem, to dare:

> *When the night of the grey Iscariots*
> *Lies dead in the red of the dawn,*
> *Queen of the scythe-wheeled chariots,*
> *Rise up, ride out, reborn!*

Both Meic Stephens and Harri Webb have been smilingly satirical about the 'pint-pot patriots' of Merthyr *a'r bro* in those days, and in some of Harri Webb's poetry there is a certain sense of 'as soon as this pub closes, the revolution starts', but in 'To Wales' there is more than a suggestion that armed resistance would not be inappropriate to the state of Wales, and it is worth remembering that the badge of the white eagle, which became the logo of the Free Wales Army and other Nationalist groups, was designed by Harri Webb, in 1952.

TRIAD is as much a manifesto as anything Harri Webb wrote in THE WELSH REPUBLICAN or WELSH NATION. Crucial to any understanding of his art as a poet is the deliberate mixture of styles and forms – lyric, ballad, satire, the intellectual, allusive poem, the scholarly translation, the drinking song. But every poem is about Wales: there is no other subject. This point was well taken by Gerald Morgan in his review of TRIAD in WELSH NATION (May, 1963):

Harri Webb is the most committed to Wales, but although he sometimes teeters on the verge between poetry and propaganda, his poetry is what we need most to counterbalance the over-seriousness of the corpus of Welsh poetry in English.

Harri Webb himself would be scornfully impatient of any concept of a *verge between poetry and propaganda*, but a shrewder point lurks below the second distinction between his poetry and the *over-seriousness* of the Anglo-Welsh poetry of the sixties. It was not until 1974 that R. S. Thomas published WHAT IS A WELSHMAN? as a riposte to those critics who regarded him as *nowhere to go for a laugh*, and the seriousness of the poetry of the sixties did border sometimes upon solemnity. The wit, the comedy, the brashness, the calculated moments of vulgarity, the salty and uninhibited assertion of Harri Webb's art disinfected the 'myth and museum' culture of his time, as it also validated his own use of Welsh history and topography and the English-language literature of his time, in poems like 'Carmarthen Coast'.

Harri Webb contributed two poems to the second publication of the Triskel Press, CANEUON RHYDDID CYMRU (Songs of Welsh Freedom) which appeared in the Summer of 1963. The first is a nostalgic 'war

53

song' in Welsh, 'Rhyfela Hyd Marw'. The second is one of his best-known ballads, 'The Cross Foxes', commemorating a mighty drinking session during the National Eisteddfod at Rhosllannerchrugog. The chorus goes:

> Hideho, Hidehi,
> In Rhosllannerchrugog we drank the pub dry.

It is the immediate, local application of an epic orgiastic incident, more characteristic of BEOWULF or the exploits of Dagda in Celtic mythology, that informs the heroic comedy of this poem, where the heroes are assembled as on the plain of windy Troy:

> From Cardiff and Rhondda and Dowlais so fair,
> The principal pinters of Gwalia were there.

The local landscape has always been a vital presence in Harri Webb's art, and its evocation in a string of place-names is a common rhetorical device, as in 'The Nightingales', who are

> singing beyond the Teifi
> By Aeron, Ystwyth, Rheidol and those secret waters
> The Beacons hold: Rhiangoll, Tarell, Crawnon . . .

The names conjure up their own importance as they are spoken. It is like Yeats saying *I write it out in a verse*, in 'Easter 1916'. The names of Wales have a potent magic for Harri Webb. It is significant that in this year, 1963, he joined a movement which became a growing interest: *Cymdeithas yr Iaith Gymraeg*.

CANEUON RHYDDID CYMRU ends with the three verses of 'Hen Wlad fy Nhadau', and in the follow-

54

ing year, after he had been appointed Librarian at Mountain Ash at a salary of £1,050 per annum, which represented his first adequate income since leaving the Navy, he published a twenty-four-page pamphlet on OUR NATIONAL ANTHEM, again with the Triskel Press. He realizes that 'Hen Wlad fy Nhadau' needs both explication and apologia:

Mr Saunders Lewis has called it 'the most lying anthem in Europe'. Somewhere between this austere verdict and the boozy hwyl *of the rugby fans, there is a feature of our national life that commands scrutiny.*

He describes the genesis of the poem (of which only a part forms the anthem) and analyses it line by line, in the manner of a painful preacher. But he makes much of its origin in an artisan's workshop. Evan James, the weaver of Pontypridd, seems to have written it in response to an invitation to emigrate to the United States to join others of his family who had gone before and done well. What gives the poem its importance and its guarantee for Harri Webb derives from the fact that it was written, rapidly, by a poet of the working-class, set to music by his son, that it arises from a real situation – it is 'factual' – and that it belongs, in every respect, not to the aristocratic, educated tradition, to the 'crachach', the 'uchelwyr' but to the 'gwerin', the common people of Wales. That is what sanctions it. The essay is dedicated to Meic Stephens, *another of Pontypridd's poets.*

Evan James wrote nothing else that anyone remembers. But he stayed in Wales. He resisted the lure of America. He wrote:

Pleidiol wyf i'm gwlad . . .

Harri Webb explains, *Pleidiol is the adjective. The noun from which it derives is Plaid*. Webb's own devotion to his country, and specifically to the valleys of south Wales which formed his *cynefin*, was expressed in his continuing membership of *Plaid Cymru*. He stood as Plaid Cymru candidate for Pontypool in the General Election of June, 1970, and polled a very respectable 2,053 votes (5.3% of the poll). It is interesting to note that Harri Webb and Meic Stephens are the only Anglo-Welsh poets to have stood as candidates in a General Election. Harri Webb's election address is vigorous, witty, irate, and it centres on the *locality*:

When I think of Wales, I think first of the raped and plundered valleys of Glamorgan and Gwent . . . I think of the people of these Valleys – the best in the world. Of the young people deprived of amenities and opportunities and forced to go away. Of the older people who remain, whose grandchildren will be forever strangers to them. I think of these things and I am angry. Not with England or the English people (there are too many of them in Plaid Cymru for that!) but with the soulless, centralised system of government that had brought these things about.

This powerful sense of *place* exercises a vast influence over both the prose and the verse of Harri Webb. His development as a poet was facilitated and encouraged by Meic Stephens. Indeed, Harri Webb would probably not have bothered to publish much of his work, except on a casual, occasional basis, had it not been for the founding, at Garth Newydd, in 1965, by Meic Stephens, of POETRY WALES, a quarterly magazine which has provided a platform for almost all the poets in Welsh and English, from that time to this. Without making him write nothing but serious poems, Stephens made Harri Webb take his poetry seriously, and they sparked ideas and poems off each other. It is not unique, individual utterance: it arises from a complex cultural context. Part of this context is provided by the characteristically Welsh tradition of the *bardd gwlad*. This movement has been fully described by W. Rhys Nicholas in THE FOLK POETS (*Writers of Wales* series, 1978), but, briefly, it is a term sometimes applied to a poet without much formal education, whose poems praise his particular locality, and the events, the births, marriages, deaths, scandals, achievements which take place there. In Welsh, such poets are masters of the traditional metres and the intricacies of *cynghanedd*, and their verses frequently appear in newspapers or *papurau bro*. Some localities, like Ffair Rhos or Llangranog, are famous for their *beirdd gwlad*, and the best known of all is probably the Cilie family of poets, descendants of Jeremiah Jones (1855–1902), who farmed Y Cilie, near Llangranog. Many a more ambitious and wide-ranging poet, in Welsh or English, has his roots in this tradition; the local in no way precludes the universal. The Welsh-language poet Waldo Williams, for example, although much of his work is erudite, devotional and deeply personal, is also, in certain ways, a *bardd gwlad*, celebrating the people and places of his native Preseli. This point is strongly made in WALDO WILLIAMS, by James Nicholas (*Writers of Wales*, 1975). Harri Webb knew and admired Waldo, and included a poem on him in A CROWN FOR BRANWEN (1974). He was also well aware of the *bardd gwlad* tradition, and memorably described a local example of it from his childhood days in Gower in his autobiographical essay 'Webb's Progress' (PLANET, 30, 1976):

. . . *another great Gower character, the laureate of our com-*

*munity, the poet and raconteur, Cyril Gwynne, also a connec-
tion by marriage and I do not know how much of an example
and a stimulus to my young imagination. I used to have many
of his cheerful, simple, rhymes, tales and musings by heart. The
giant mangel-Wurzel, The Hungry Lurcher, What's in a name?
Feyther mightn't Like it – the titles tell you all about them. I
retained a fondness for them throughout the years of Ronsard
and Baudelaire and all the other giants, a fondness which
unfortunately had outlasted all but a few fragments in my
memory. And he established in my mind the image of the poet
as essentially a social rather than a solitary character, one
moreover, fortunate in his gifts, however humble, and under
something of an obligation to spread them around for the
pleasure of the people he belongs to, rather than to hoard them
in the dank private cellars of introspection and incomprehension.*

The difference, of course, is *the years of Ronsard and
Baudelaire and all the other giants*, the extended and
intensive education which not only equipped Harri
Webb to range widely in European literature, but
fostered in him the scholarly habits of study without
diminishing his intellectual curiosity. Cyril Gwynne
could never have translated Pablo Neruda's ALTURAS
DE MACCHU PICCHU into Welsh: Harri Webb did. Yet
in 'Not to be used for babies', a poem first published
in POETRY WALES (3.1., 1967), he writes, factually, of
a strictly local character perfectly in the tradition of
the *bardd gwlad*:

> *Old Glyn, our milkman, came from down the country
> Between Waunarlwydd and Mynydd Bach y Glo,
> A neighbour of innumerable uncles and cousins
> In an untidy region of marsh and pasture and mines . . .*

That is how the poem starts, but it develops into a
reminiscence of the golden days of boyhood, before
ending starkly:

I buy my milk in a tin.
It is a dry powder. They have ground Glyn's bones.

The *bardd gwlad* tradition, like the holy localities of the south Wales valleys, are a source and a starting-point out of which the deeper resonances of many of the poems develop.

Between 1965 and 1973, when Meic Stephens relinquished the editorship, Harri Webb published his poems steadily in POETRY WALES. Meic Stephens moved out of Garth Newydd in 1965 and, newly married, went to live in another part of Merthyr. Harri Webb went on living alone in the empty rooms of the old house, contributed occasionally to the political debate, became a member of the English-language section of Yr Academi Gymreig, and conscientiously carried out the duties of Librarian of Mountain Ash. He wrote articles and reviews for WELSH NATION during these years, and published the occasional poem in the WESTERN MAIL and elsewhere, but it is in the pages of POETRY WALES that one may see his bewildering variety of styles emerge. He contributed to every issue in the first five years, sometimes one poem, sometimes several, and this brought him before the poetry-reading public of Wales and beyond as a writer quite different from the political journalist of THE WELSH REPUBLICAN, or the propagandist of the Plaid.

THE GREEN DESERT: COLLECTED POEMS 1950–1969 was published by Gwasg Gomer, Llandysul, in 1969, and it brought together fifty-two poems, the great majority of which had appeared in print before. Eight of the eleven poems from TRIAD are reprinted, together with almost all the poems contributed to POETRY

WALES. Poems which had first appeared in CILMERI are reprinted here, together with a few which first saw the light of day in newspapers. Apart from the very light and ephemeral verse, THE GREEN DESERT brings together almost all the poetry Harri Webb had written, and considering that he was forty-nine years of age when the volume appeared, he cannot be said to have been a prolific poet. It caused some surprise to its first reviewers and subsequent critics. Belinda Humfrey, in THE ANGLO-WELSH REVIEW (21.48, Winter 1972), was prepared to give him the benefit of her doubt:

. . . perhaps his unifying theme of Wales can be cited as a justification for the astonishing higgledy-piggledy of serious poems and trivial verses in his volume, or manifesto, of twenty years collecting . . .

She was clearly taken aback by such a collision of the serious and the trivial but her instinct was right in seeking a justification in the relentlessly focused 'unifying theme': Wales. The higgledy-piggledy seems not to have astonished the more perceptive reviewer, Ioan Bowen Rees, who writes in POETRY WALES (5.3, 1970):

Few of Harri Webb's poems are not about Wales and few of those about Wales are not about Welsh nationalism . . . even in this age of petty specialisation, the politician really is a poet.

He sees clearly that the Anglo-Welsh poet has to build a special relationship with his audience:

. . . he has to get off his pedestal and go into the pub, be the opposite of 'tall and unpopular'. It is a great thing for the future of poetry, of common culture and of sense of community that so

much of Harri Webb's verse is immediate, witty, rhythmical, committed and, for all his deep knowledge of the roots of Wales, accessible.

In phrase after phrase in this brief review, Rees gets it right:

The sociability of much of Harri Webb's verse is itself very much in the 'centuries older' Welsh tradition which he admires . . . the epigrams are pure Sarnicol . . . Harri Webb's technical versatility, his wit, profundity and scorn, his sense of history, his 'gift for the memorable phrase' –

> *They fought well among their native forests*
> *But fighting retail were beaten wholesale.*

The true distinction is not between 'serious poems and trivial verses', but between the *bardd gwlad*, as exemplified in 'Epitaph on a Public Man' or 'Lines Written in a Country Churchyard', and the student of *Ronsard and Baudelaire and all the other giants*, who wrote 'Sestina in November' and 'The Nightingales'. It is perhaps indicative of the general seriousness and solemnity of Anglo-Welsh poetry in the 1960s that anyone should find Harri Webb's vast variety of subject, tone and style astonishing, at a time which elsewhere saw, unastonished, the flourishing of Adrian Henri, Brian Patten and Roger McGough, and which witnessed the emergence of John Betjeman as Poet Laureate.

The title Harri Webb gave to this collection is richly ambiguous and crucial to an understanding of the poems. To the non-Welsh reader THE GREEN DESERT carries a distant echo from Eliot's 'Waste Land' as a judgemental statement about contemporary Wales; it is a wry oxymoron, in that green is the Celtic colour, and the colour of fertility and fecundity. Deserts ought to be brown. But it is also the colloquial name given now in Wales to the sparsely inhabited upland area in the Cambrian Mountains between, say, Tregaron and Carno, the last vast emptiness at the heart of Wales. Harri Webb seems to have been the inventor of the phrase 'the green desert' to describe this area, as he invented several other now accepted colloquial names (he may well have been the first to describe north-Walians as 'Gogs'). As a symbol it has a double significance. The green desert is bleak, forbidding, thinly populated, unproductive save for a few sheep and the massed hordes of conifers planted by the Forestry Commission and a handful of entrepreneurial Englishmen rich enough to be attracted by the tax concessions, and to this extent it can stand for the exploited, invaded, sheepish and diluted culture and society which Harri Webb found rampant and regnant in his nation. But, at the same time, the desert which is green is a remote, inaccessible place, a forbidden country to those who do not understand its ways and its language, where things grow new, undetected, unexploited, and where a nation can cherish itself, the deepest parts of itself, in a natural and creative silence. Harri Webb illustrates the symbolism in the last lines of 'The Boomerang in the Parlour', a poem about his father's emigration to Australia:

> Terra incognita: *a land whose memory*
> *Has not begun, whose past has been forgotten*
> *But for a clutter of nightmares and legends and lies.*
> *This land, too, has a desert at its heart.*

It is the same impulse as that which drew R. S.

Thomas, at much the same time, to the hills and the moors of Cefn Coch, above Adfa, to the harsh and unfertile hills, Mynydd y Gribyn and Y Glonc, where he felt the truth was to be found in the uncultivated acres and utterances of Iago Prytherch.

Following the title page, and opposite the details of publication, stands a dedicatory epigraph which, like its predecessor in TRIAD, is meant to make a point:

> *Grevose est la guere, e dure a l'endurer:*
> *Quant aillours est l'este en Gales est yver.*
> *Pierre de Langtoft*

Langtoft is a village in Yorkshire, and Peter of Langtoft was probably a canon of Bridlington who lived in the reigns of Edward I and Edward II. THE CHRONICLE OF PIERRE DE LANGTOFT , IN FRENCH VERSE, FROM THE EARLIEST PERIOD TO THE DEATH OF KING EDWARD I, was translated into English by Robert of Brunne, and both versions were edited for the Rolls Series by Thomas Wright in 1868. The couplet occurs in vol. ii, p. 176, in the entry for 'anno domini 1282', where Pierre shows himself to be strongly prejudiced in favour of Edward I and hostile to Llywelyn. Robert translates it:

> *Grievous is the war, and hard the suffering;*
> *When elsewhere it is summer, it is winter in Wales.*

So, in the very front and forehead of this 'higgledy-piggledy' collection of poems stands this haunting couplet from a forgotten medieval chronicle written by a Yorkshire monk who regarded the Welsh as troublesome rebels threatening the peace and order of the realm. The couplet stands there not simply as a piece of showing off, Harri Webb parading his learning (though it is that), but as a marvellously poised and ironic comment both on the contemporary state of 'the green desert' of Wales and on the poems which follow in the volume. The first of these, 'A Loyal Address' had been previously published in TRIAD under the title 'To Wales'. It begins:

> Queen of the rains and sorrows,
> Of the steep and broken ways,
> Lady of our to-morrows,
> Redeem your yesterdays.

In TRIAD the title led one to assume that it was addressed to some mythical imaginary queen of Wales who is likened, in the final stanza, to Boudicca, Queen of the Iceni. The change of title seems odd, and can perhaps only be explained by the reference in a set of brief manuscript notes which Harri Webb made (probably in the late seventies or early eighties) on the poems in THE GREEN DESERT and A CROWN FOR BRANWEN, and which survive in the archive now in the care of Meic Stephens. A propos of this poem Webb writes 'A Loyal Address: Prompted by the coronation of Elizabeth II, 1953, Later in the volume there appears his 'Song for July':

> The cockerel crows in the morning,
> The lark sings high at noon,
> The blackbird whistles the sun down
> And the owl cries out to the moon.
>
> We must make do with their music
> For the birds of Safaddan are dumb:
> They only sing for the rightful Prince
> And he has not yet come.

The manuscript notes in the archive record *'Song for July: My Investiture poem'*. In the blinding light of hindsight one can perceive in both poems a subtle web of ironic reference directed, in each case, to enforcing the point that the House of Windsor has no relevance to the nation of Wales, which remains a sovereign nation waiting for its true rulers to arise and emerge. This sense is deeply latent in the poems, not dominant, and it may be no more than a codified sub-text, working on allusions available only to the *cognoscenti* who are privileged to be inward with the poet's beliefs and ideals. No contemporary reviewer seems to have picked up the point, and it may be that the poems are less than wholly successful on that account. But the existence of such a reticulation of ironies should warn us that the poems in this collection are unlikely to be as unsubtle as some of them seem.

Harri Webb's manuscript notes on his poems, used circumspectly, throw light on certain aspects of many of them, which may aid understanding, though they may in some cases prejudice critical appraisal. It might be argued that if the poems need the notes then they fail as poems – though that approach would have to contend with Eliot's first publication of 'The Waste Land'.

Some of the notes add interesting information, about the occasion of the poem, or the poet's method of work. Of the light, and seemingly slight, poem 'A Whisper' he writes:

This is part of my reaction to the Plaid Cymru victory in Carmarthen in 1966. The other two poems inspired by that event were 'Colli Iaith', and a ballad 'When Gwynfor got in for

Carmarthen', which had some currency until he was got out again in 1970. This is the negative side.

'Colli Iaith' is, of course, in the opinion of many, the poem above all others by which Harri Webb will be remembered, but the ballad appeared in WELSH NATION in September 1966, and was not reprinted until A CROWN FOR BRANWEN (1974). It is interesting, though not important, and possibly distracting, to hear what the poet says about 'Valley Winter':

Written in and about Merthyr in the late 50s. The legendary unpunctuality of Merthyr's municipal bus service, which is referred to in the last-but-one line, was in fact the starting point of this poem, and it reflects also the political atmosphere of the time.

His comments on the next poem, 'Local Boy' are more illuminating, and helpful:

Begun *as a Christmas card for K.[eidrych] R.[hys] 1960? but developed its own impetus. Sent to him privately and not really intended for publication, but published by him in* WALES *and became popular. Not a religious poem.*

The last sentence removes any possibility of misunderstanding about intention, and the first shows how this poem, like many another, developed a life of its own.

The note on 'Not to be used for Babies' offers an insight into the poet's methods of work, interesting because it is presumably not characteristic:

Written in just about as long as it takes to write it down, one Saturday morning in Garth Newydd, after a late breakfast of repulsive instant coffee and dried milk. Written on the dining

66

table without clearing away the breakfast things. Worked on later, of course, but not much change needed.

Most of the notes offer information additional to the poems, though the information added to 'Synopsis of the Great Welsh Novel' is unusual for its reticence, its obliquity and its unwillingness to wound even in this manuscript-and-private place:

It would be unkind to specify who exactly I was getting at here. The student of the A.[nglo] W.[elsh] novel will know, and the general reader won't want to. I am getting at a genre, not individuals, and more than that, at a wider habit of thought about Wales. Perhaps it is not really a 'literary' poem at all.

Clearly, he envisages his readership as including 'inside' groups, like the students of the Anglo-Welsh novel, as well as a more general public, so that the poem is available on at least two levels. This 'coterie', insider element in his writing is vitally important, and a definitive quality of his art, where the surface simplicity and 'readability' often conceals a deeper direction and intention. This is easily illustrated, and close to the surface, in 'Epitaph on a Public Man' (see p.61). It is a neat epigram, in the respectable tradition from Martial through Ben Jonson and the Jacobean epigrammatists. It could apply to anyone. But the suspicion is alerted in the reader's mind that the poem refers to some particular person in Welsh public life, and speculation is encouraged as to who it might be, with no shortage of candidates at either national or local level. Incidentally, Harri Webb's manuscript note on the poem ends immediate conjecture: *It refers specifically to Dr Thomas Jones, C.H.*

Throughout his notes Harri Webb is insistent that his

poems are 'factual'. It is important to him to register that the events actually happened as described, that the description is accurate, that the incident really did occur, that the character existed. This is best illustrated by his comments on 'The Antennae of the Race':

This episode took place in December 1941 off the West Coast of Scotland. I had been just three days at sea, as had much of the ship's Co[mpany]. The ship was a Hunt Class Destroyer HMS Tetcott, and we were in collision with a corvette HMS Heartsease (previously christened Pansy, but changed for obvious reasons, known to the matelots as Heart Disease). The radar crew's full names were Les Ikin, Nick Buckovski and Les Ball.

All this adds absolutely nothing to the understanding or appreciation of the poem, but the poet seems to want the actuality, the historicity of the amusing but unimportant event to be 'on the record'. It is as if he is saying 'I'm not making it up; it's true, you can ask Les Ikin or Nick Buckovski or Les Ball if you don't believe me'.

The same almost hectoring insistence occurs in the note on 'The Hill' and 'Thanks in Winter':

Both poems are quite factual. There is nothing 'contrived' about them. It is the plain truth that 'the day that Eliot died I stood / by Dafydd's grave'. It's something one would hardly forget, and it demanded to be written about – January 1965.

This view of poetic creativity is quite unlike that expressed by Shakespeare in A MIDSUMMER NIGHT'S DREAM:

> The poet's eye, in a fine frenzy rolling,
> Doth glance from heaven to earth, and earth to heaven;
> And, as imagination bodies forth
> The forms of things unknown, the poet's pen
> Turns them to shapes, and gives to airy nothing
> A local habitation and a name.

Harri Webb's concern with the concrete, the historical event (whether yesterday or a thousand years ago), the striving to be faithful to the facts and to create a 'record' are what make him, essentially and inescapably, a political poet.

Oddly enough, for one so concerned with truth, Harri Webb seems less anxious for verbal accuracy, and he sat very lightly to the disciplines of proofreading. THE GREEN DESERT contains many misprints, which remain uncorrected in the third impression, although the manuscript notes make one interesting emendation to the poem 'April in the Suburbs':

> Blind to all the springtime's graces
> Deaf to all the wild bird's calls
> With leather coats and leather faces
> Beefy bags bash little balls.

That is the reading of the printed text. The notes comment, casually:

Inspired specifically by a glimpse of those grotesque creatures (it should be hags *not* bags*) on the golf-course at Rhiwbina.*

The poem itself is sub-Betjeman, and one of the few in the collection which might be thought a due recipient of Belinda Humfrey's astonishment. Yet other poems, which appear slight, deserve the praise

69

due to perfect examples of their (minor) kind. As an epigram, the 'Lines Written in a Country Churchyard' carries exactly the right weight and depth:

> Who says that our nation
> Does not honour its poets?
> Is not Dafydd ap Gwilym
> Buried in the same sacred spot
> As Sir David James?

The gesture towards Thomas Gray in the title reminds us of his 'mute inglorious Miltons', most readers (even in England) would be at least vaguely aware that Dafydd ap Gwilym was a Welsh medieval poet, but far fewer would recognize now the name and significance of Sir David James (1887–1967). He was, as THE OXFORD COMPANION TO THE LITERATURE OF WALES records,

the benefactor of numerous good causes and institutions, including the eisteddfod held annually in his native village of Pontrhydfendigaid, Cards. He made a fortune from business interest in London . . . He was buried in the churchyard at Strata Florida (Ystrad Fflur) not far from the yew-tree which is said to mark the grave of Dafydd ap Gwilym.

What prestige this confers upon the rotted poet!

The two finest poems in the collection are successful for quite different reasons. 'The Sailor and the Sundial' is simply a brilliant brief narrative poem, explaining the fury of a drunken sailor outside a pub against a sundial on the opposite wall, which

> Established, immovable on the old stone wall
> Looked down its long aristocratic gnomon and
> With elegant, indolent economy, conned the sun.

70

The 'wit' of it would have been acknowledged by John Donne. 'The Stone Face', by contrast, is a wholly serious and 'literary' poem on the sculptured stone head, possibly of Llywelyn Fawr, dug up at Deganwy in 1966. The buried head, the severed head, the carved stone head, are powerfully potent symbols in Celtic history and mythology, and the poem lives up to the tradition in which it is written.

THE GREEN DESERT is sparsely populated. The poet himself is the principal presence, and things are seen from his point of view. Harri Webb is not a dramatic poet in the sense that he often and easily assumes a persona other than his own. Perhaps the central poem in the collection, in that it clearly proclaims its deepest themes and unites them in the key, geographical image which gives the book its title, is 'Above Tregaron'. It commemorates a journey taken with Phil Williams in the early sixties along the Abergwesyn Road, an old drovers' road which had only recently been metalled, which runs between Tregaron and Beulah, over the loneliest part of the 'green desert' between the rivers Irfon and Camddwr. In these silent spaces

> *you are as far away*
> *As you will ever be from the world's madness.*

Yet this is not a poem of retreat, of nostalgia, *à la recherche du temps perdu*:

> *Flying from madness, maybe we bring it with us,*
> *Patronising romantics, envying the last survivors*
> *Of an old way of life, projecting our dreams*
> *On this conveniently empty scenery, deserted*
> *By its sons for the hard bright streets we come from.*

The success of THE GREEN DESERT established Harri Webb as a poet of stature in Wales, and one who should be watched as his development proceeded. In the period 1969–74 his poems found their way regularly into the literary magazines like PLANET, ANGLO-WELSH REVIEW, SECOND AEON, and especially, POETRY WALES. He continued to publish poems in the Plaid's newspaper, *Welsh Nation*, for which he also wrote regular political articles. There were reviews, literary articles, translations, letters to the editor, and the like in Welsh papers and magazines, and an increasing number of these were in the Welsh language.

IV

The early 1970s contained little in the way of outward incident in Harri Webb's life. After his failure to win the Pontypool seat at the General Election he never stood for Parliament again. He continued as Librarian for Mountain Ash, applied (unsuccessfully) for a post at the College of Librarianship, Aberystwyth, attended a symposium there on libraries and the arts in September, 1969, which may have been the basis for his LIBRARIES AND THE ARTS, an address delivered to the Conference of Library Authorities in Wales at Brecon on Tuesday, 8 June, 1971, and published at Mountain Ash by the author later in that year. He was obviously proud of this piece, and rightly so. It is a serious and sensible contribution to the subject, and displays a sensitive understanding of what it is possible and practical for a library service to undertake.

In 1971 he renewed contact with some members of his family at a poetry reading in Swansea, and a recording of THE GREEN DESERT was released by Cambrian Records, Pontardawe. It was well reviewed in POETRY WALES (8.2., Autumn, 1972) by John Stuart Williams, who made a shrewd point:

If I happen to prefer Ray Smith's reading to that of Margaret John it is only because I feel that, whatever else may be said, Harri Webb's verse is better served by a man's voice. It works by assertion rather than by suggestion and Ray Smith's delivery supports its driving rhetoric well.

In 1972 he moved to a rented house, 2 Rose Row, Cwmbach, in the Cynon valley, and spent three weeks in Canada at the expense of the Welsh Arts Council. He had been a co-opted member of the Council's Literature Committee since 1970, and contributed many memoranda on matters concerning the Council's support of Literature in Wales. It may well have seemed that the rampaging republican rebel of the earlier years was settling down into harmless respectability like so many of his middle-aged countrymen did, and do, having done (as they see it) their 'bit for Wales'.

Any such appearance would have been deceptive. Outward quiescence was not matched by any such serenity of mind. In his political articles he continued to beat the Nationalist drum as before, and observers would have detected few changes in his attitudes. But his ideas *were* changing, silently, privately, and his political thought moved in a new direction towards an extreme position.

This is clear from an unpublished letter to Gwilym Prys-Davies, from which I have been generously permitted by the recipient to quote at some length. It is, indeed, a very long letter – almost an essay – and it provides a unique insight into Webb's inmost thinking in the first half of the 1970s. From internal evidence, it was written at some time in March or April, 1972, and it begins with a *raison d'être*:

. . . I felt it necessary to put down on paper a clarification of my attitude and to offer a critique of yours. I have been doing this with various people, by letters and in conversation for some time, and it has always produced some sort of results.

He is distressed by the spiritual lethargy of the nation:

. . . one of the things that has been and still is wrong with the Blaid – they are cold-blooded – or at least the people who have set the tone in the Blaid do not seem to possess any capacity for judging the emotional reactions of people. All the faults both of the Blaid and the Labour Party stem from the unhealthy state of the nation – the 'pacifism' of the Blaid – which is not the strenuous non-violence of Gandhi but merely a polite name for lack of moral fibre, and the sheer scoundrelism of the average local Labour Party are both characteristics of a nation which has reached rock bottom . . .

He looks to history for an explanation of this condition:

I see the idea of national sovereignty and independence as something that has been safeguarded by different strata of society, and as one class has fallen, another has stepped in. I think the line of descent from the princes, via the rebel chieftains, the gentry, the middle-class of the eighteenth century right down to the Gwerin is pretty clear and unarguable. What we must face now is that the last of these social bulwarks has fallen. The Gwerin has given up . . . The Republican failure could perhaps have been foreseen in any case, it was definitive, final. But it contained the seeds of renewal. If it brought one phase of Welsh history to an end, it began another. We saw then the Gwerin's final rejection of Wales. We saw also, the assumption, by a few individuals of an unparalleled responsibility. As Legonna wrote in the W[elsh] R[epublican] 'we set ourselves apart as founding fathers'.

The consequences which flow from this are new and remarkable in Harri Webb's thinking:

To these men, in this age, has the sovereignty of Wales fallen. They and no other are the Welsh nation. The others have sunk so low, are so deeply stained with the guilt of servitude that their condition may be likened (as Pearse likened it) to that original sin in which theologians say the human race is lost. The act of redemption can only come through the sacrifice if necessary – and I believe it to be necessary of the lives of the best. This I think goes beyond the old Republican doctrine. The Republicans said that they would not accept the self-imposed trammels of pacifism with which the Blaid leadership disguised its lack of moral fibre. The Republicans said that they would not shrink from shedding blood if necessary. They said that bloodshed would probably *be necessary. I say now, that such sacrifice is not only* probably *necessary, a predictable statistical likelihood, but ABSOLUTELY NECESSARY. Without it there will be no wholeness or health in any of the other actions that lead us forward. It is necessary, first, to redeem the Welsh from shame . . .*

Padraic Pearse's doctrine of the necessity for 'blood sacrifice' to redeem and liberate Ireland was a most powerful and influential belief, based on the need for the Irish to lay down their own lives in the struggle for freedom as an atonement and a ransom for the craven failures of their forefathers. It was analogous to the redeeming sacrifice of Christ on the cross to atone for human sin. The whole argument in Harri Webb's letter shows him moving to the same point. And he is quite clear about the consequences:

Today, although only on the fringes of things like that, I am quite psychologically prepared for anything – jail, disruption of personal life, hardship, the lot. I am on active service. I have been called up.

Harri Webb had personal experience of active service and knew what it entailed. The letter reads like a grave, serious personal commitment to struggle for the political freedom of Wales at whatever cost. The only vehicle for action, for all its defects, was Plaid

Cymru, and he mentions the major problem which its pusillanimous pacifism caused him:

I straight away found myself in the anti-leadership group in the Blaid who were pressing for a much firmer line; people to whom the offer by the Blaid of compromise proposals over Tryweryn, and the failure to take action after Tryweryn were a betrayal of that particular cause and of the national cause.

It seems clear that at this time, if at no other, he was ready to die for Wales.

Yet this was precisely the period when he was making plans to swan off to Canada, at the expense of the Welsh Arts Council, for three weeks of cultural conversations and comparisons, which might reasonably be expected to include a little alcoholic refreshment and *a mess of boon companions to spend the evenings* (see p.74). There might even be a *roomful of pretty girls*. The contradiction is not evidence of hypocrisy, but of complexity. In the early 1970s Plaid Cymru was the *only* real nationalist organization. The Republicans had failed, and the 'New Nation' movement did not survive long enough to be weaned. Canada, and particularly the province of Quebec, offered a potential model for the future of Wales. Contrary to appearances, the visit had a serious purpose. The cause of Welsh Nationalism had to be pursued at the international level. It is against this background that we must judge poems in his next volume, A CROWN FOR BRANWEN, like 'Marwnad for Drums', 'For Franz Fanon', and especially the brief 'Advice to a Young Poet':

> *Sing for Wales or shut your trap*
> *All the rest's a load of crap.*

On the reorganization of local government in 1974 Harri Webb, to the surprise of many, retired prematurely from the library service with a lump sum and a pension he considered modest but sufficient. He was fifty-four. He continued to live in Cwmbach, and in the same year he published with Gomer Press A CROWN FOR BRANWEN, which collected most of the poems he had written since THE GREEN DESERT in 1969. The book is well-produced, and granted the dignity of hard covers and a dust jacket,which is appropriate for what is the most important, characteristic, and 'heavyweight' collection of Harri Webb's poetry. Glyn Evans, reviewing it in Y CYMRO (4.2.1975), went immediately to the heart of the matter:

Bardd gwladgarol yw Harri Webb yn anad dim ac mae amryw o gerddi cenedlaetholgar yn y casgliad hwn.

(Harri Webb is a patriotic poet above all, and several of his nationalist poems are to be found in this collection.)

All the poems spring from a patriotic impulse, all are based on, or refer to, or come round to Wales, and this central, obsessive, implacable subject is, as usual, approached from a dazzling variety of angles. This is not a fact potently perceived and presented by Peter Elfed Lewis in his long, solemn and careful review for POETRY WALES (10.4). He compares the book with Gwyn Williams's FOUNDATION STOCK, which, he finds, 'has its ups-and-downs', though

. . . they are not nearly as yo-yo like as those of A Crown for Branwen, which is a kind of Poetry All-Sorts.

This is the heart and soul of Mr Lewis's approach.

78

He is concerned to dissect the collection and preserve 'his best work' for posterity's praise, while consigning 'his least convincing' to the dustbin of his disapprobation. He ends:

But, oh, how much more impressive as a whole this book would have been if Harri Webb had taken an axe to it and lopped off at least fifteen pages of dead wood.

To be fair, Mr Lewis does come to realize that the book has a central thrust and purpose, even if his discovery does not strike him with all the force of an epiphany:

. . . the initial impression of a poetic potpourri is qualified to some extent by the sense of genuine commitment to Wales that lies behind the book . . . In the circumstances 'anthology' may not be an inappropriate description after all – in the sense that, however diverse the book is stylistically, it does have a central and unifying theme, Wales.

Stylistic diversity makes Mr Lewis uneasy, as he shows when he describes the contents of the book:

It contains one poem in Wlesh [sic.]; translations from Welsh, Breton, and Martiniquais; an imitation or adaption (not a translation in the orthodox sense) of one of Dafydd ap Gwilym's best-known poems; a small group of parodies; poems in free, blank verse, and poems in very strict forms (such as a sestina, 'Saraband'; a poem in octosyllabic couplets, 'Thoughts in an Area of Outstanding Natural Beauty'; and a number of poems in quatrains, mostly the abab kind); poems from two lines in length to about fifty; poems from three to a page to one occupying three pages. The sheer variety is astonishing, so that at first sight the book looks like a somewhat bizarre anthology rather than the work of one man.

This is an accurate and useful description of what A CROWN FOR BRANWEN contains. But there is more to it than that. Once again, it is worth taking up the hint provided by the epigraph, a brief quotation from Geoffrey of Monmouth: *Est etenim vester / nam quondam praelia vestra / vestrorumque ducum cecinit.*

Typically, Harri Webb provides no context. The implication would be that the lines come from the HISTORIA BRITONUM, but in fact they do not. They are taken from the final paragraph of the VITA MERLINI, the Life of Merlin (ed. Basil Clarke, Cardiff, University of Wales Press, 1973, pp.134–5), where, after the great vision of the prophetess has reached its climax, Geoffrey himself, as it were 'signs off':

We have bought the song to an end. So, Britons, give a laurel wreath to Geoffrey of Monmouth. He is indeed your Geoffrey, for he once sang of your battles and those of your princes, and he wrote a book which is now known as the 'Deeds of the Britons' – and they are celebrated throughout the world.

In this coded, oblique, allusive and scholarly gesture Harri Webb is equating himself with Geoffrey and claiming that his poetry too sings of the battles of the Britons, and their deeds *celebrata per orbem*.

Wales is certainly the central and unifying theme, but what Harri Webb celebrates is the variousness, the diversity, the universality, and the integrity of Wales. The jewel has many facets, and the poems light up the facets in many ways – by juxtaposing and contrasting the comic and the serious, the present and the deep mythological past, small and large, light and profound, the technically highly-wrought and the casual and easy, the popular and the scholarly, the personal and the impersonal, even the Welsh language and the English. For example, the collection opens with 'Penillion':

> *Colli iaith a cholli urddas*
> *Colli awen, colli barddas*
> *Colli coron aur cymdeithas*
> *Ac yn eu lle cael bratiaith fas . . .*

Oddly, this is the poem by which Harri Webb is probably best known in Wales. It was set to music by Meredydd Evans, sung everywhere, and its fame spread rapidly especially amongst Welsh-speaking patriots. It deals with present events, it is brief (twenty short lines), it is direct, popular, impersonal, and in Welsh. The second poem is an entire contrast. 'A Crown for Branwen' interprets an image from the 1940s by reference to Branwen, the daughter of Llŷr in the Second Branch of PEDAIR CAINC Y MABINOGI deep in the mists of the past. It is more than twice as long as 'Penillion', it is indirect and allusive, with a certain élitist intellectual difficulty, it is highly personal and it is written in free verse and in English. The poet's unpublished manuscript notes recall that readers have found difficulty with this poem, and he offers a considerable commentary, which begins (as so often) by asserting the fact:

. . . there really was a huge anti-tank trench across the south of England in the invasion scared period of 1940–41. I used to see it from the Downs, hitch-hiking up from Fareham & Portsmouth on leave. It was called the Ironside Line & plans of its general line are to be found in books dealing with the period . . . It was not, of course, until much later, the early 50s, that it coalesced in my mind as an appropriate image for certain aspects of the role of the Anglo-Welsh writer in modern Wales, which the reader must of course deduce for himself . . . Why

Branwen? Briefly, because she was an unfortunate princess whose story still has the power to move the heart, & the name in euphonious . . .

He sees that the Writers of Wales must be a tank-trap against the English invasion in his own day, and he offers this image, this insight, to the mythological princess who fell from greatness to misery and died of grief at Aber Alaw because she had failed to reconcile two warring nations. The poet John Ormond, reviewing the collection in the WESTERN MAIL (5 August 1974) saw the importance of the poem to the book:

Like all true poems, it cannot be paraphrased; and, as such, it is the heart, the intensely-worked keystone of the book.

The poem makes the point that is made again in the later 'Our Scientists are Working on it' (*Poems and Points*, p.33):

> What Wales needs, and has always lacked most
> Is, instead of an eastern boundary, an East Coast.

Ireland, of course, has an East Coast. And an Irish Republican Army. The later poem leaves little implicit in its sense of the need for Welsh resistance. But the danger is apparent enough in 'A Crown for Branwen'.

The third poem in the volume retreats almost out of sight of the political immediacies. It is a virtuoso piece, 'Saraband', in sestina form. It is technically brilliant, but most readers, while admiring the art, are at a loss to know what the poem is about. Harri Webb's notes reveal all:

It is a reminiscence of the Northern Lights as I used to see them when stationed at Wetherby at the end of the War, flickering over the Plain of York, and, therefore, of course, over the battlefield of Catraeth.

The fact that, in this case, the note is vital to an understanding of the poem is a sufficient verdict on the poem. It is a scintillating failure. But the first three poems are deliberately drastically different from one another, and they are ambitious in quite separate ways.

The next two poems, 'Postcard from Llanrwst' and 'Abbey Cwmhir' are simpler and less venturesome. They form a linked pair of narratives about Welsh heroes, Llywelyn the Great in one case, Llywelyn the Last in the other, connected by the image of a coffin and contrasted by the geographies of Llanrwst and Cwmhir. The judgement, in each case, is that the people of Wales have failed to keep faith with the heroes of its history, and, in Harri Webb's view, this is the great betrayal, the deepest treachery. It would be difficult to overestimate the importance of this theme in all Harri Webb's work, either in verse or in prose. The concept of *brad*, treachery, is as complex as it is heinous; it involves deliberate treason, of course, but it includes neglect, disprising, careless and slothful forgetfulness of one's inheritance; it is as much a sin of omission as commission. The first poem in his 1977 collection, RAMPAGE AND REVEL, is entitled 'Cofiwch' (*Remember*), and it begins:

> *Boed i Gymru ailgofio y dyddiau a fu*
> *Cyn i'w meibion ei bradychu . . .*

As he said in the letter to Gwilym Prys-Davies:

The Gwerin has given up . . . We saw then the Gwerin's final rejection of Wales . . . It is also, for myself, a phase in the progress towards commitment which I see to be the chief need in Wales today . . .

Faithlessness, *bradwriaeth*, is a theme which runs like a thread through A CROWN FOR BRANWEN through 'A True Story', 'To a Reader', 'A Voice in the Wind' (where Aneurin Bevan is 'A Silurian prince who lost his way), 'The Meeting', 'Thoughts in an Area of Outstanding Natural Beauty', 'The Emigrants' and particularly in 'Now', a poem of which he says in his manuscript notes:

This is the sort of poem that the Anglo-Welsh literary magazines will publish! And who am I to disagree with them?

Superficially, it is an amusing commentary on Welsh hypocrisy, but the roll-call of the heroes and heroines of the mythological past, the Arthurian pantheon culminates in a recognition:

> *But there's one of them*
> *Who's still very much with us. Yes, you've guessed,*
> *It's Medrawd.*

Medrawd (or Medraut, Medrod, or Mordred) was, according to the ANNALES CAMBRIAE, a hero who died with Arthur at the battle of Camlan and for many of the old Welsh poets he was an example of courage. Geoffrey of Monmouth, however, portrayed him as a traitor to Arthur. In Book X (2) of the HISTORIA Arthur leaves to fight Lucius Hiberius, and gives the charge of defending Britain to his nephew

Mordred and his Queen Guenevere. But Mordred (X. 13) tyrannously and traitorously usurped the crown and *linked him in unhallowed union with Guenevere the Queen in despite of her former marriage.* Arthur returned, defeated Mordred at Winchester, and finally killed him at the river Camel in Cornwall. Harri Webb's poem, a light, satirical review of the vanished Arthurian past, can still locate one Arthurian character in modern Wales: the traitor. Violence lies close to the surface. 'Briefing' begins:

> *Come down from the high horse. For a space let him canter*
> *With tossing mane over the mountains. This is a job*
> *That must be finished on foot, with a short knife . . .*

The poem proceeds with instructions for pursuing some dangerous beast into a cave, and killing it in hand-to-hand combat. Harri Webb's manuscript notes add:

The original of this version was more savage and inciting . . . The Minotaur is of course John Bull.

It is, perhaps, imperceptive of critics to be so dazzled by the 'higgledy-piggledy', the 'potpourri', the 'anthology' element in both THE GREEN DESERT and A CROWN FOR BRANWEN that they fail to detect the serious Nationalist intention, the often savage critique of his countrymen, the steady approach to the political position he seems to have espoused by the middle of the 1970s, the realization that nothing will be achieved in the struggle for Welsh freedom until a dedicated élite group arises, who are ready to shed blood (their own first) for their country's cause.

Yet the comatose critic may easily be pardoned. The

message is deeply and carefully encoded – mostly in comedy. There are poems which, openly or obliquely, are written 'in praise of Wales': 'Acquaintance', 'Where?', 'Day Out', or 'Harri Webb to Harri Vaughan' where he writes:

> To you our rivers sang of bliss
> Beyond all mortal pales,
> I ask no other heaven than this,
> My paradise is Wales.

And almost half the volume is comedy. From a wistful redaction of the story of the Nativity ('Never Again'), to 'The Next Village to Manafon' (with its unspoken commentary on the world of R. S. Thomas) through the brilliant invention of 'Continent Isolated', which begins:

> There was a Fog in our pub the other night.
> He trailed his native element with him. Fog
> Came out of his ears, when he opened his mouth
> What came up was pure Fogspeak . . .

and ends:

> Don't forget, none of them foreigners have got
> A Royal Foggily. As he went out
> All the foghorns sounded for him on the other side.

The translations from Welsh poets, ancient and modern, are perhaps the weakest things in the volume, and one would question Harri Webb's success as a translator were it not for the splendid and a scabrous 'version' of Dafydd ap Gwilym's 'Diweirdeb Merched Llanbadarn':

> *Talk about chocker, I could spit.*
> *To hell with all the judies here,*
> *I'm randy and can't get a bit.*
> *Will they drop 'em? No bloody fear . . .*

Harri Webb's commentary in his notes is enlightening:

Done in about 1972. Unpublishable, of course, in the 'poetry' magazines. Recited by Ray Handy, dressed in trendy Carnaby Street – Kings Road gear, in the satirical 'Nails' programme on HTV in 1973. Objected to at rehearsal and had to be specially 'cleared'. Criticised in the WELSH NATION *as deliberately dirtying the sacred memory of pure, stainless Dafydd.*

If there is a touch of *bardd gwlad* parish-pump parochialism about the 'Three Parodies' towards the end of the volume it is redeemed by the sheer skill and satirical incisiveness, and the parodied poets (John Tripp, Gillian Clarke and R. S. Thomas) have long since pardoned him.

The comic poems, and the satire, won critical acclaim. Perhaps this sort of thing was what the reviewers had come to expect from Harri Webb. He seemed to be essentially the Jester, the Fool to Wales's King Lear, licensed to sting though not to damage, and, as such, capable of being recognized, praised, understood and assimilated by the *uchelwyr*, the *crachach* of the Welsh Literary Establishment. But the comedy in A CROWN FOR BRANWEN was nothing new. The tone and the topics had been evident and little changed since TRIAD. What was new was the scarcely concealed violence, the challenge to action, the call for 'commitment'. He was expected to write funny poems about Jim Griffiths ('The Old Leader').

He was not expected to translate and publish 'Marwnad for Drums' from the Martiniquais of Auguste Macouba, a poem given to him by Paol Keineg (see PLANET, 7, Aug.–Sept. 1971):

> Memory is living, growing,
> Their blood has dried on the walls
> And in the streets of death
> And on their murderers' hands.
> Their blood is a voice that remembers,
> And your blood, our murdered brothers,
> Is ours who live.

This theme, which unites Padraic Pearse, John Jenkins, Keineg, Macouba, the Stern Gang and Franz Fanon was new, and not attractive to the critics. They ignored it.

A CROWN FOR BRANWEN marks an extreme point in Harri Webb's development as a writer. From being, in his earlier years, an optimistic, cheerful Welsh Republican he had moved through various stations of disillusion to the point where he was ready to hint in print that only the blood sacrifice would be a full, perfect, and sufficient sacrifice, oblation, and satisfaction, for the sins of his countrymen. This position was simply not tenable. He must have realized this in or about 1975. It was clear that Plaid Cymru was not going to rouse the nation to direct action or armed revolt. The Free Wales Army had come and gone, and terrified no one. The joke, well-known in the Lampeter area, asked 'How many are there in the FWA?', and the answer was 'either twelve or thirteen depending on whether you count Cayo Evans's dog in or out. Most people count him in, because he's the most intelligent of the lot'. The commander of a local

Army Cadet Force dared the FWA to a pitched battle. The offer was not taken up. Similarly, there was no point in looking for aid from across the Irish Sea. The power available to the well-organized Republican movement in Ireland, the resources and experience of Sinn Fein and the Irish Republican Army, were obviously not replicable in Wales. Guerrilla warfare in the Brecon Beacons was out of the question, and the overwhelming majority of Welsh people simply didn't want to know. A little light cottage-burning involving selected, empty, English-owned second homes was the absolute limit to which a very tiny number of patriots was prepared to go. The future must have looked bleak to a man in his mid-fifties, and his realization that the *gwerin* had betrayed Wales, that the country was at rock bottom, and that we who had *set ourselves apart as founding fathers* of the new Republic had attracted no followers and begotten no offspring, must have been a bitter enlightment.

In 1974, after a gap of more than twenty years, he resumed the keeping of his journal. This journal (currently in the keeping of Meic Stephens) records his disenchantments. After retiring from the library service he had invested a large part of his meagre capital in Triban, a trading company set up by Plaid Cymru members. There was no scandal, no negligence, no corruption, but the company failed to prosper. By the time it was wound up Harri Webb had lost several thousand pounds. As his letters make clear, he was convinced that he had been duped, exploited, taken for a ride; and he resented it deeply and bitterly. This loss seems to have been crucial in the souring of his attitude to the Plaid and for the bitterness with which he writes about particular individuals in his journal. It is significant that he published very little poetry in the period immediately after A CROWN FOR BRANWEN but he did contribute a translation of the first Manifesto of Cymdeithas yr Iaith Gymraeg, originally drafted by Cynog Dafis, in PLANET (26–7, 1974, pp.77–136).

The sour coincidence of his ideological and financial troubles made some action imperative. He needed money, and it was a help when the Welsh Arts Council commissioned him to compile a report on publishing in Wales. He delivered parts of this, but never completed it. He found himself gradually being taken up by 'the media'. He had always been an able, professional journalist, and in 1975 he began writing the Preview column in RADIO TIMES, a commitment he maintained for some five years. He also made substantial contributions to the television series *Poems and Pints* which began a long, popular run on BBC Wales. He became *bardd teledu*, a television poet.

It was during the 1970s that Harri Webb became quite a skilled and successful television and radio script-writer. He was never formally trained for the trade, nor did he ever work in the television industry, but he developed a very recognizable style which was popular in Wales and beyond. *The Waves around Wales* is a typical radio-script (broadcast on 16 January 1976), using four voices to perform what is in effect a dramatic ballad interspersed with music and sound effects. After fifteen seconds of music from the Second movement of *Sea Sketches* by Grace Williams it begins:

> *A land of mountains, yes, but a land also*
> *Knowing the sea;*

> *And of our four frontiers, only one*
> *Is a green dyke . . .*

It is unambitious and simple, and it gains its very considerable effect by allowing words and sounds to stir the imagination – as all good radio writing should.

His television scripts are more technically ambitious. The most successful is undoubtedly *How Green was my Father* (broadcast by BBC Wales, 1975), a film satire on life in the valleys, which tells the story of a third-generation Yankee Taffy who comes home to search for his roots and tries, incidentally, to rediscover 'the spirit of the valleys'. It was written with one particular actor in mind, Ryan Davies, who gave a *tour de force* performance, playing all fourteen characters, with only Max Boyce as a supporting actor punctuating the story at odd moments like a 'Greek chorus'. Ryan Davies, as a 'Hell's Angel', directs the Yank to the registers of the local school:

Aye, old Basher Belsen 'ave got piles of registers. Goes back hundreds of years they do. Right back to Ramsay Macdonald's time . . .

The screenplay is clever and complex, involving dream sequences and any number of surreal effects, and the visual comedy complements the verbal, as when the Yank's enormous 'stretch limousine' draws away, revealing a very long bus-queue.

Not everything he wrote was accepted for production. A typescript survives of *Big Deal*, a modern version of the Crucifixion, told from the standpoint of the Roman soldiers (one of whom is a recruit from

Wales), which contains a great deal of fine comedy, but was obviously a shade too sensitive for the times (1977). Among several rejection letters is one from Granada Television:

We found it an interesting and affecting piece of writing though I'm afraid that it is not a play that we would wish to produce. I should perhaps let you know that I have already received a number of modern versions of the Crucifixion during the last couple of years.

It is a delicate refusal, and reveals that Harri Webb seems not to have made use of any literary agents in publishing his work, either for the media scripts or for the verse and prose. For better or worse, he marketed his own products.

The corollary of this is that he had to produce poems to go with the act. He must write poems for performance, for the stage rather than the page. They must make an instant impact, and they must be broadly acceptable to a wide audience whose principal interests were far from literary. In short, he had to write poetry to order, and give the public what it wanted.

He had done so before. 'MS found in a Bottle' was written shortly before it was put out on the Welsh Arts Council's Dial-a-Poem service, and Harri Webb's manuscript note records:

The seamanlike vocabulary was vetted by ladies with cut-glass accents in the Arts Council offices & passed as Fit for Transmission. But of course it caused 'offence' . . .

Conversely, those notes record a few hints that he

had become increasingly restless with the 'literary magazines' in which he had previously published. He writes of his fine poem 'That Summer':

It is an accurate transcription of what are literally my first significant memories. When POETRY WALES *refused to publish it, I lost interest in the magazine.*

Editors of poetry magazines have a hard time and do strange things, but it may well have been experiences like these which turned Harri Webb's mind more and more towards poetry as a 'performance art'. Certainly, the performances helped to keep the wolf from the door and his name in the public prints. The publishers' blurb to his 1977 collection, RAMPAGE AND REVEL illustrates the new directions in which his life was moving:

. . . His work is among the favourite material of acclaimed actors Ray Smith and Philip Madoc, choirs as diverse as Côr Meibion Menlli and Cantorion Cynwrig, popular groups like Triban and The Hennesys, and such attractive young singers as Olwen Rees and Heather Jones, who scored a hit with her single of his 'Colli Iaith'.

Harri Webb's own introduction to the volume makes the point that the poems in it are of a different kind from his previously published work:

Nearly all of these poems, songs and ballads were written for performance rather than reading. They deal for the most part, and light-heartedly as often as not, with the more extravert and active side of our national history and character, and are arranged, more or less, in chronological order, for want of a better.

All the poems in RAMPAGE AND REVEL could be

described as songs or ballads without straining either term, though some ('Sweetapple Fair', 'The Stars of Mexico' or 'The Absolute End') might be difficult to set to music. Although many of them are narratives, telling, in the simplest way, great stories from Welsh history ('Princess Gwenllian', 'The Raid of Ifor Bach', 'The Women of Fishguard'), the collection includes a song in praise of the Cardiff City Association Football team which won the FA Cup in 1927, and an account of the Cardiff versus Newport Rugby Union match played in March, 1975. Harri Webb's manuscript notes on the poems in this collection are, for the most part, laconic to the point of being virtually dismissive, but they make it clear that the poems date from the early 1960s to just before publication, and they are assembled on no single observable principle, save only the ever-present fact that they are all concerned with Wales. The first poem (one of two in Welsh) is the earliest. Harri Webb writes:

Written in 1961, a year in which I was particularly prolific in throw-away pieces (The Cross Foxes, etc.). It is a close copy of 'Let Erin Remember' and must be sung to the same tune. I have heard it to other tunes, which only confirms my positiveness on this point . . . I had it with me at the National Eisteddfod at Rhosllannerchrugog (Hei di ho, hei di hi!) & various words I was short of were put in by such diverse collaborators as Neil Jenkins & Donal Mullins (not yet then a bishop).

His insistence on the tune illustrates the importance he now gave to the performance of his work. There are thirty-five poems in RAMPAGE AND REVEL and an analysis of Harri Webb's notes to them reveals, tellingly, the shift in the sources of his 'poetic inspiration'. Seven of them ('The Black Ships', 'Strange Craft', 'A Tall Story', 'The Voyage of the

Dragon', 'The Pirate King', 'Gower Smugglers' and 'Three Men of the Sea') were specifically written for a programme called *The Waves around Wales*, broadcast in 1976. Eleven others ('Princess Gwenllian', 'The Raid of Ifor Bach', 'The Battle of Berwyn', 'Prince Llewelyn', 'Cestyll y Cymry', 'Owain Glyndŵr', 'The Merthyr Rising', 'Rebecca and her Daughters', 'To the Shores of Patagonia', 'The Long Strike' and 'Penyberth') were deliberately written for a projected set of twelve Nationalist ballads to be issued as a Long Playing Record. The scheme came to nothing because of *the incapacity of musicians*. Another programme, called *Song of the River*, included 'The Merthyr Rising' plus four new poems written specially for it ('Sweetapple Fair', 'The Girl on Pen-y-Fan', 'The Lady, the Minstrel and the Knight' and 'The Bluebirds'). *Song of the River* also included 'The Iron Steed', which was not written specifically for it, but was one of two (the other being 'Guto Nyth Bran') of which Harri Webb writes:

I wrote this with the intention of circulating it [to] schools in Mountain Ash, but nobody was interested. Early 1970s.

Thus, twenty-four of the thirty-five poems were commissioned or written to order, or written for schools. Several of the remaining eleven were included simply as 'fillers'. He says of 'Christmas Cheer':

I am rather surprised at the inclusion of this piece. I don't think it has all that much going for it, & only put it in to make up numbers. Written during one of my last Christmases at Garth Newydd.

Of 'The Love Spoon' he writes:

Commissioned by Glenys James of Pontypridd, as promotional material for one of her lines: replica lovespoons in Brass! I think I got £10 for it. About 1972–4.

Circa 1967 he had written ambivalently, ironically, about the beneficence of the Welsh Arts Council in 'Cywydd o Fawl' (in THE GREEN DESERT, p.43):

> *Praise let them be for this thing,*
> *Money they are distributing*
> *Like Beibil Moses his manna*
> *Tongue we all, bards Welsh, Ta!*

Times change, we all move on, everyone has to earn a living, but there has been a sea-change between the Harri Webb who wrote the passionate pamphlet about Dic Penderyn and the Merthyr Rising of 1831, and the balladeer who wrote, lamely, of the same events in 'The Merthyr Rising' in RAMPAGE AND REVEL:

> *. . . But soldiers kept on coming,*
> *We met them face to face*
> *Unarmed outside the Castle Inn,*
> *The masters' meeting place.*
>
> *And at the masters' harsh command*
> *They fired on the crowd,*
> *And all the gutters ran with blood.*
> *Why are such things allowed?*

Even the rhythm and the metre (control of metre has never been Harri Webb's greatest accomplishment) break down, and the rhymes dictate the writing. In RAMPAGE AND REVEL he had become, in some ways like his mentor Hugh MacDiarmid, the people's poet, in that his poems were heard by, and briefly known to, a wider and vaster audience than ever before in his lifetime as a writer. But he paid a heavy price for that achievement.

Between 1977 and 1983 he continued as an active and industrious reviewer, translator, journalist, broadcaster, scriptwriter and popular poet. In 1977 he went with Meic Stephens on a visit to Rennes in Brittany to take part in a conference of Celtic peoples at the Maison de la Culture, and the tour included a trip to Mont St Michel. Strangely, in view of his interest in the language and the culture, it seems to have been Harri Webb's first visit to metropolitan France since a trip to Paris as a schoolboy.

At home, he continued to maintain a reasonably active public life as journalist and entertainer. The WESTERN MAIL had described him as 'the uncrowned poet laureate of Wales', and he did not disavow the accolade. In the spring of 1978 he took part in the series *Fy Newis i* on BBC Cymru, choosing seven pieces of his favourite music and readings to punctuate an interview. It was not exactly *Desert Island Discs*, but it kept him in the public eye. His choice, incidentally, ran from Bach's 'Jesu, Joy of Man's Desiring', through Smetana's 'Vltava' and Saunders Lewis's 'Pendefig Duw' to the second movement of Bruch's Violin Concerto.

In 1980 he made his will. He named his half-brother Michael Webb, as his executor, and Meic Stephens his literary executor. He bequeathed his body to the Department of Anatomy at the University of Wales Hospital. On 6 October he made what seems in some ways the ultimate renunciation for him: he gave up alcohol completely. It was as if he were preparing to fold his tent and silently steal away. Yet the following year saw him greatly in demand for public readings, and highly praised for his performances. He made many appearances with a new colleague, Eiry Palfrey, who seems to have exerted a strongly life-enhancing influence upon him.

In 1983 he brought out his fourth, and last, slim volume of poems, POEMS AND POINTS. Like the previous three, it was published by Gomer Press (Gwasg Gomer) at Llandysul, a small but highly efficient printing and publishing house which has served the writers of Wales since 1892. It has published almost all the important Welsh authors of the twentieth century, and, in one form or another, it has been responsible for presenting the work of all the Anglo-Welsh poets since the Second World War to a growing readership. Its imprimatur is very much a mark of distinction. The cover design of POEMS AND POINTS is a shrewd guide to its contents. It depicts St David, in bishop's robes, with crosier and mitre, in the act of drop-kicking a hydrogen bomb out to sea and between the rugby posts set up on a desert island. The particular allusion is to the last poem in the collection, 'A Sermon on St David's Day', commemorating the dropping of the first H-bomb on Bikini Atoll, on 1 March 1954. The rest of the collection brings together many of the 'performance' poems from the public readings and programmes like *Poems and Pints*, together with a few originating elsewhere.

Some of the ballads seize on the political events of the moment. 'History and Prophecy', for example, comments on the bewildering shifts in the Conservative Government's Energy policy:

> They want coal again and they want the men
> Who'll go down the hole and cut it,
> But the miners' lads have asked their dads,
> And they've told them where they can put it.
>
> Our English friends are at their wits' ends,
> For fuel they're in trouble,
> For they sank their brass in North Sea gas,
> And that was North Sea Bubble . . .

The poet is not above including a strict Shakespearean sonnet on the general political scene, which begins:

> Season of mists and party conferences
> At off-peak rates in moribund resorts . . .

There is a bleak and characteristic comment, in his old allusive style, on the current state of the nation in the aptly-titled 'Holm Rule', a poem inspired by the island, Flat Holm, in the Bristol Channel:

> All hail the island Utopia
> You can see from Penarth Pier,
> Flat as its name, uncontoured,
> No history . . .
>
> Ideal republic, democracy
> And dictatorship here may agree.
> Only one person lives there, it's said,
> And he's dead.

But the one poem which stands out from all the others is his brilliant verdict on the Thatcherite years, and the Government's determination to ensure that 'competition' is forced into every crack and orifice of national life: 'Tristes Tropiques'. It tells the story of a courtesy call by HMS *Truculent* to a South Sea island. The crew introduce the happy natives to Association Football. The natives take it up, and excel at it, but, since *Competition / Was not in their culture*, they ensured every game was drawn:

> *All the sailors*
> *Marvelled at their play, their mastery of football.*
> *A pity, they said, they've missed the point*
> > > *completely.*

> *All that co-ordination, strength, skill, control,*
> *And they play every match for a draw. It was a waste of time*
> *Us teaching them the game in the first place. But there,*
> *What can you expect from a lot of primitive savages?*

Some of the poems are much less successful, but there is one oddity which gives an oblique insight into Harri Webb's activities in the 1980s. Under the title 'Wider Still and Wider (Translations made at the Rotterdam International Poetry Conference)' he offers the original of his famous 'Ode to the Severn Bridge':

> *Two lands at last connected*
> *Across the waters wide*
> *And all the tolls collected*
> *On the English side.*

followed by translations into Irish (Michael O Huanachain), Breton (by Per-Jakez Hélias), Dutch (by Leo Neilssen), Castillan (by Homeros), French (by Jean-Clarence Lambert) and Serbo-Croat (by Jana Beranova). Clearly, he was now widely recognized as 'a poet of Wales', sent on the international conference circuit from time to time, and befriended by poets of other countries.

There is just a hint, here and there in the collection, of the deep grievance of the 1970s, *bradwriaeth y werin*, the betrayal of Wales by its own people, as in the brief poem, 'Redevelopment':

> *Twice have I seen my native town*
> *By wrath and greed to ruin brought down,*
> *Once from the sky by those called Huns,*
> *And once again by her own sons.*

POEMS AND POINTS is the least overtly nationalist of Harri Webb's publications. He is as anti-English as ever, but without the earlier sense of outrage, that sense that something must be done, the determination to rouse his countrymen to action. The lot of the convinced Welsh nationalist in the early 1980s was not easy: it was a hard row to hoe.

Earlier in 1983 occurred the strangest coincidence of the poet Harri Webb with a public event in Wales. He was invited, or commissioned, to write words appropriate to be spoken on the occasion of the Official Opening of St David's Hall, Cardiff, *in the gracious presence of Her Majesty Queen Elizabeth The Queen Mother*. It is a strange poem which the old Welsh Republican wrote. It even incorporates one of the verses, 'The Art of the Possible' from POEMS AND POINTS, and follows it with the lines:

> *From the past of a people*
> *Content with little,*
> *Creating great art*
> *Out of the simplest, subtlest of instruments,*
> *The human voice,*
> *We stand now*

> On the threshold of a new age,
> Where everything is possible . . .

But as we know from the work of John Betjeman or Ted Hughes it must be difficult to be a poet laureate – crowned or uncrowned.

His final book was a prose work, TALES FROM WALES, retold by Harri Webb, and illustrated by Lesley Bruce. It was published in London, by Dragon Books, in 1984. It contains little to interest anyone who has read Harri Webb's earlier work, but it does form a good and easily assimilable introduction to some traditional Welsh stories for anyone unacquainted with them.

On Tuesday, 2 April, 1985 the WESTERN MAIL published an interview between the journalist Mario Basini and Harri Webb. Not too much should be made of it. Harri Webb was in very poor health at the time, and it may well be that he said things, for dramatic effect, which he would not otherwise have said. Entitled 'English? That's the dying language', it begins with an announcement:

The man who made his reputation as the 'enfant terrible' of the English language literary scene in Wales has just struck a blow for what he sees as the nation's only real language. He has stopped writing.

This is true, of course. But if he had given up writing in English (his first language, and the language in which he had written almost everything he wrote) it was because he had given up *writing*. He had no more to say. Mr Basini develops the theme, and his quotations from Harri Webb show the old poet characteristically at his most provocative, outrageous and controversial:

'I don't believe that writing in English about Wales matters very much any more', he says. 'Anglo-Welsh literature is, more or less, a load of old rubbish. It has only marginal relevance to Wales now.' It is English, not Welsh, he sees as the dying language. 'When I learned French I realised that there was no future for English. It is not a language at all, really. Unlike Welsh . . .'

The interview deals sensitively with Harri Webb's political dreams and visions, which, by 1985, seemed so unlikely to blossom into reality. Basini writes:

He makes no pretence about his political stance as a nationalist. But his commitment is tempered by an awareness of the difficulties of his position.

And he quotes Harri Webb's comment in reply:

'All nationalists are idolators. They offend against the Second Commandment – "Thou shalt not make unto thyself graven images." They place their country alongside God. But when you look around for alternatives, there aren't any.'

This final comment, as witty as it is illogical, is where Harri Webb's political thinking comes to rest. The strange thing is the association in his mind of God with politics. God (who is, and always has been important to him, though the only place he writes about it is in 'Webb's Progress', in PLANET, 30 (1976), pp.23–28) is placed 'alongside' his country. This would imply that his country is the idol, the false God. But this is not quite what Harri Webb means. At all events, he has been true to his word. Since

1985 he has not published anything significant, except his sonnet on Dowlais (see p.32).

On 30 October 1985 he suffered a stroke or a seizure, and was taken to the Prince Charles Hospital in Merthyr, where he remained, seriously ill, for about six months. There followed a period of convalescence in the Mardy Hospital in Merthyr. Soon after his return he moved from Rose Row to Bryn Hir, Cwmbach, where Mrs Betty Phillips acted as his house-keeper, and Councillor Glyn Owen (a friend of long standing) managed his financial affairs. And he lives there still. He sees few of his old friends now, except for Meic Stephens, and one or two others, spending most of his day watching television and reading reference-books.

There have been several critical assessments of the poetry of Harri Webb (Belinda Humfrey, ANGLO-WELSH REVIEW, 21, 1972; C. B. O'Neill, ANGLO-WELSH REVIEW, 65, 1979; Tony Curtis, in WALES: THE IMA-GINED NATION, 1986; Mercer Simpson, POETRY WALES, 23.2–3, 1988; Nigel Jenkins, PLANET, 83, 1990). There has even been a teaching pack, issued by the Clwyd Centre for Educational Technology, featuring ten poems, notes, and twelve colour-slides. His strengths and weaknesses as a poet have been analysed, truculently or generously, but always with care and judgement.

But it is altogether too early to give any comprehensive verdict on Harri Webb as one of the Writers of Wales. Like Milton, there is vastly more of him in prose than there is verse. At all events, the evidence in the case has never yet been assembled. Before any proper judgement can be attempted there must be a volume of his COLLECTED POEMS with notes or an interpretative introduction. His political journalism must be brought together and at least a representative selection must be made available to the reader. Quite apart from their social and historical value, many of his pieces in THE WELSH REPUBLICAN or WELSH NATION are still topical and funny enough to amuse a readership interested in the satirical and scurrilous – and any publisher would be unlikely to encounter libel suits at this distance of time. His vast correspondence must be collected, since so much of his serious political thinking was done in letters, in collaboration with people like Legonna, Gwilym Prys-Davies, Emrys Roberts, Meic Stephens, and many others with interests in the Nationalist cause from the end of the war to the present day. There are, to say the least, many hundreds of letters, to Harri Webb and from him, in the National Library or in private hands, which, taken together, will provide radical new insights into the plotting and planning of left-wing Nationalists in Wales from 1950s onwards. For example, Harri Webb writes to an unknown recipient in an incomplete and undated letter (*c.* 1953):

The real work is not to state on paper or in the privacy of our political confessionals that we are now members of the Labour Party, but just to get out and be members of the Labour Party . . . The full programme is not to 'join the Labour Party' but to join the Labour Party and take it over . . .

Such infiltrationist tactics, such utopian dreams of achieving political power, proved all too illusory; but they were seriously dreamt.

Similarly, in an undated letter written from Garth

Newydd sometime in the early 1960s to Gwilym Prys-Davies, he says:

At the moment P.C.'s loc. govt policy is substantially to support the present system with a few obviously necessary improvements & to say 'We'll work it better than the other lot.' This is a totally inadequate policy for a nationalist movement. I hope to change it . . . There is one other point I want seriously to take up with you and that is your rejection of the argument for the blood sacrifice. I know it is a sensitive subject, one which should not be mentioned lightly or discussed with anything but the utmost seriousness . . .

He moves without difficulty from consideration of bureaucratic and administrative reform in local government to the necessity for armed and violent rebellion for the freedom of Wales. Such letters, and there are so many of them, are a source which must be critically investigated before any proper assessment can be attempted.

Above all, there is his Journal. This incomplete, rambling, vast and voluminous, illegible archive of his vagrant life, sometimes turgid, morbid, desultory, piddling and dull, sometimes deeply personal and revelatory, and occasionally profoundly meditative, has hardly ever been read, except by Meic Stephens, let alone evaluated. He could have destroyed it. He chose to retain it in his literary archive, and, apart from its biographical interest, it casts a continuous commentary on his written work, whether in prose or verse.

In one long, rambling sequence, written when he was on shore-duty near Derna, in Libya, in March 1943, he writes about Swansea, about Dylan Thomas, about his own attitude to the craft and sullen art of writing. While on watch, he notices

The MTBs coming in in the evening, the Corvettes going out, watching them till they were lost in the clouds to sight; no sunsets [like those on] the sea. I said to myself: sapphire shallows, purple deeps, but looking again I think it's the other way about. But juggling & consciencelessness are part of the art of poetry, so I must not be too serious about that . . .

Many thousands of words later he speculates on what he might be doing after the war:

The spectre of graduate unemployment in England after the war, is, in Libya during what I suppose will be looked back on as the Great Lull, precisely – a spectre. The situation will have to be considered in detail when it presents itself. In the meanwhile, I have cleared my mind of a lot of bedfluff. I must not expect life to be too picturesque.

The Journal, and the mass of other unpublished, manuscript material in Harri Webb's archive, comprise a vitally important background for a full understanding of his life and his thought. And his published work cannot be critically evaluated until they are taken fully into account.

He is unlikely to publish anything else. Asked about this, recently, he said 'I have spoke my speak', and could offer nothing more than what he had said to Mario Basini in 1985. Appreciation of his art is in its infancy; his stock will surely rise as he comes to be seen as a great purveyor of life, laughter, optimism and indefatigable energy in a period of Welsh history characterized by the exact opposites of those qualities. The annals of activity in Wales have seldom been more torpid than they have since 1950, but the Welsh nation, like the statue of the Dying Gaul in the Museo Capitolino in Rome, is still there. As Harri Webb said to Mario Basini:

Wales is still there. It is up to us what we do with it.

He himself has always been much like his hero, Hugh MacDiarmid, who described himself thus in 'A Drunk Man Looks at the Thistle':

> *I lauch to see my crazy little brain*
> *– And ither folks' – tak'n itsel' seriously,*
> *And in a sudden lowe o' fun my saul*
> *Blinks dozent as the owl I ken't to be.*
>
> *I'll ha'e nae hauf-way hoose, but aye be whaur*
> *Extremes meet – it's the only way I ken*
> *To dodge the curst conceit o' bein' richt*
> *That damns the vast majority o' men.*

Whaur extremes meet describes Harri Webb well. In a sense, all his dreams, all his political thought and work, have come to nothing. There is no Workers' Republic of Wales, nor is there like to be; there is no devolution from English rule; Plaid Cymru continues the same as ever; the Welsh language is just about holding its own. But he would not see it in that way. To him, the struggle goes on; sooner or later the nation will be free. *If it be not to come, it will be now; if it be not now, yet it will come: the readiness is all.* The dominant quality in that final interview with Mario Basini is Hope. Hope springs eternal in Harri Webb's breast, and though he may have despaired of the *gwerin* he has never lost his Faith in Wales. Faith and Hope characterize all his writing, and to these we may add the third Pauline virtue of Charity. In the true sense of the Latin *caritas*, love, it is Charity towards God, his country and his fellow man, which has always been at the heart of Harri Webb.

Glyn Owen tells the story of Harri, quite recently, going with him as usual to church for the 8 a.m. service of Holy Communion. He required walking sticks and Glyn's support to make his painful way to the altar rails at the appropriate moment. As they knelt, Glyn noticed that Harri's trouser leg had ridden up, exposing a length of white leg, and drew his attention to it. Harri turned with difficulty, surveyed the situation, and eventually rectified it. As he straightened, he felt a powerful twinge. 'Bloody hell', he said, fervently and audibly, then turned and raised his hands to receive into them the body and blood of Christ.

A Selected Bibliography

The definitive bibliography of Harri Webb will shortly be published in John Harris's Bibliography of Anglo-Welsh Literature. I include here only his separately published books, a guide to his journalistic work, and a few of the critical articles on his work. John Harris's work will soon make this list redundant, and the curious reader should consult it as soon as it appears in print.

HARRI WEBB

Books

DIC PENDERYN AND THE MERTHYR RISING OF 1831, Swansea, Gwasg Penderyn, 1956, 16pp.

TRIAD: THIRTY THREE POEMS by Peter Griffith, Meic Stephens, Harri Webb: with an introduction by Anthony Conran. Merthyr Tydfil, Triskel Press, 1963. 58pp. Eleven poems by Harri Webb, pp.45–57.

OUR NATIONAL ANTHEM: SOME OBSERVATIONS ON 'HEN WLAD FY NHADAU', Merthyr Tydfil, Triskel Press, 1964. 24pp.

THE GREEN DESERT: COLLECTED POEMS, 1950–1969, Llandysul, Gwasg Gomer, 1969, 74pp.

LIBRARIES AND THE ARTS: an address delivered to the Conference of Library Authorities in Wales at Brecon on Tuesday 8 June 1971. (Mountain Ash: the author), 1971. 9pp.

A CROWN FOR BRANWEN, Llandysul, Gwasg Gomer, 1974. 76pp.

RAMPAGE AND REVEL, Llandysul, Gomer Press, 1977. 63pp.

WORDS WRITTEN ON THE OCCASION FOR THE OFFICIAL OPENING OF ST DAVID'S HALL, CARDIFF, in the gracious presence of Her Majesty Queen Elizabeth, The Queen Mother. Cardiff, 1983. 4pp.

POEMS AND POINTS, Llandysul, Gomer Press, 1983. 43pp.

TALES FROM WALES, retold by Harri Webb; illustrated by Lesley Bruce. London, Dragon Books, 1984. 95pp.

A CROWN FOR BRANWEN; wood engraving by Yvonne Skargon. Newtown, Gwasg Gregynog, 1989. 4pp. (Beirdd Gregynog; Gregynog poets; 5). Text of single poem.

Journalism and Editorship

THE WELSH REPUBLICAN: Y GWERINIAETHWR, 1–7, 1950/51 – 1956/57. Harri Webb was successively managing editor, general editor and editor of THE WELSH REPUBLICAN. He also wrote a great deal of it, either in signed articles or anonymously.

WELSH NATION. Harri Webb edited this, the official newpaper of Plaid Cymru, from 1961 to 1964. He also wrote many of the satirical articles in it, often under the name John Spang.

CRITICAL ARTICLES

Bianchi, Tony, 'Propaganda'r prydydd', Y FANER, 27 Ion/Jan 1978, 9–11, 13. (A poet's propaganda).

Curtis, Tony, 'Grafting the Sour to Sweetness: Anglo-Welsh poetry in the last twenty-five years', in WALES THE IMAGINED NATION: STUDIES IN CULTURAL AND NATIONAL IDENTITY, ed. Tony Curtis, Bridgend, Poetry Wales Press, 1986, pp.99–126.

Humfrey, Belinda, 'Harri Webb in the Wrong Language', ANGLO-WELSH REVIEW, 21, 48 (1972) 9–17.

Jenkins, Nigel, 'The Poetry of Harri Webb', PLANET 83 (1990) 18–23.

Jones, Sally Roberts, 'A Matter of Choices: the Poetry of Harri Webb', POETRY WALES, 26.2 (1990) 27–30.

O'Neill, C. B., 'Harri Webb and Nationalist Poetry', ANGLO-WELSH REVIEW, 65 (1979) 90–99. Including a bibliography covering records and broadcasts.

Simpson, Mercer, 'Harri Webb, poetic canvasser or rebel joker?' POETRY WALES, 23, 2–3 (1988) 37–40.

Stephens, Meic, 'The Garth Newydd Years: halcyon days in Merthyr', PLANET 83 (1990) 18–23.

Tripp, John, 'Harri Webb' in CONTEMPORARY POETS, ed. James Vinson. 2nd. ed. London, St James Press; New York, St Martin's Press, 1975. pp.1640–41.

Wilks, Ivor, 'Harri's Web: Harri Webb and Welsh republicanism', PLANET 83 (1990) 13–17.

Acknowledgements

Without the assistance and advice of Meic Stephens this book could never have been written. As Harri Webb's literary executor Mr Stephens has assembled and arranged a most extensive archive of Webb's papers and material relating to him, to which he has given me unrestricted access, together with invaluable guidance based on his personal friendship with Harri Webb over a very long period. I am deeply grateful to him for all his help.

I am grateful too to Lord Prys-Davies for the opportunity he provided to consult books and documents in his personal collection, as well as for many stimulating discussions on Welsh Republicanism, politics and society in Wales in the post-war period, and his own reminiscences of Webb's life and work.

A particular debt of gratitude is owed to my old friend Admiral Sir David Williams, for his assistance in tracing Webb's career in the Royal Navy, and for his astonishing memory of the warships and shore bases of the Second World War. For special help I am also indebted to Councillor Glyn Owen, Mr Selwyn Williams, Profesor R. Geraint Gruffydd, Dr Nicole Crossley-Holland, to the Librarian and staff of the Cardiff Public Library, and to the Librarian and staff of the Public Library of Merthyr Tydfil.

The Author

BRIAN MORRIS was born in Cardiff in 1930 and educated at Cardiff High School and Worcester College, Oxford. He taught English Literature at the universities of Oxford, Birmingham, Reading and York before becoming Professor of English Literature at Sheffield University (1971–80) and Principal of St David's University College, Lampeter (1980–91). He was made a life peer in 1990, and is currently Opposition Deputy Chief Whip in the House of Lords, and Chairman of the Prince of Wales's Institute of Architecture.

He has published three volumes of poetry, TIDE RACE (1976), STONES IN THE BROOK (1978) and DEAR TOKENS (1987). He was for many years general editor of the New Mermaid Drama series and the New Arden Shakespeare.

Designed by Jeff Clements
Typesetting by National Library of Wales, Aberystwyth,
in 11pt Palatino and printed in Great Britain by
Qualitex Printing Limited, Cardiff, 1993.

British Library Cataloguing in Publication Data.

A catalogue record for this book is available from the British
Library.

ISBN 0-7083-1225-X

The Publishers wish to acknowledge the financial assistance of
the Welsh Arts Council towards the cost of producing this
volume.